The World of a Mountain

THE WORLD OF A
MOUNTAIN

WILLIAM CONDRY

With line drawings by
Wilhelmina Mary Guymer

FABER AND FABER
3 QUEEN SQUARE LONDON

First published in 1977
by Faber and Faber Limited
3 Queen Square London WCI
Printed in Great Britain by
BAS Printers Limited, Over Wallop, Hampshire

British Library Cataloguing in Publication Data

Condry, William
The world of a mountain.
1. Mountain ecology—Juvenile literature
I. Title   II. Guymer, Wilhelmina Mary
574.5'264   QH541.5.M65

ISBN 0-571-10779-6

Contents

Illustrations

PLATES

ILLUSTRATIONS

FIGURES

The author thanks Wilhelmina Mary Guymer for her attractive drawings; Professor C. Kidson and staff of the Geography Department, University College of Wales, Aberystwyth for valued assistance over mapping; Derek Baylis of the Forestry Commission for guide sketches and helpful suggestions; David James for advice on the bibliography; and Vera and Robert Tushingham for mountaineering information.

1. Which Way to the Mountains?

The best way to find out what a mountain is like is to go and climb one. And in the British Isles we're lucky. We have plenty of mountains to choose from and they come in all sizes up to the 1,343 metres (4,406 feet) of Ben Nevis. You will also find a great variety of rock on our mountains. Some are sandstone, some are limestone, some are slate; others are granite or are a mixture of various rocks. Some mountains are sharper than others. Some are wetter. Some are bleaker. Most of them are in groups but a few stand apart. Some have much plant and animal life on them, others are nearly barren. Some are smooth and dry to walk on. Others are boggy, tussocky or rough with stones. But you need to experience as many different types of mountain as you can if you are going to get a real understanding of what life on our uplands is all about.

Before you decide which mountain to climb first it will be a good idea to make a mountain map, for there's nothing like drawing your own maps to teach yourself where places are. At first you might decide to mark on a map of the British Isles all the peaks over 1,000 metres (3300 feet). If you do you will find that except for Snowdon in North Wales these are all in Scotland. So to make your map of the uplands more complete it would be better to include all the ground higher than, say, 500 metres (1640 feet). Then your map would look like Fig. 1.

A fact that will stand out clearly from your map is that the mountains of the British Isles are all in the north or west. Draw a line from east Yorkshire to east Devon, curving it round west of the Midland Plain, and you will have roughly divided the British Isles

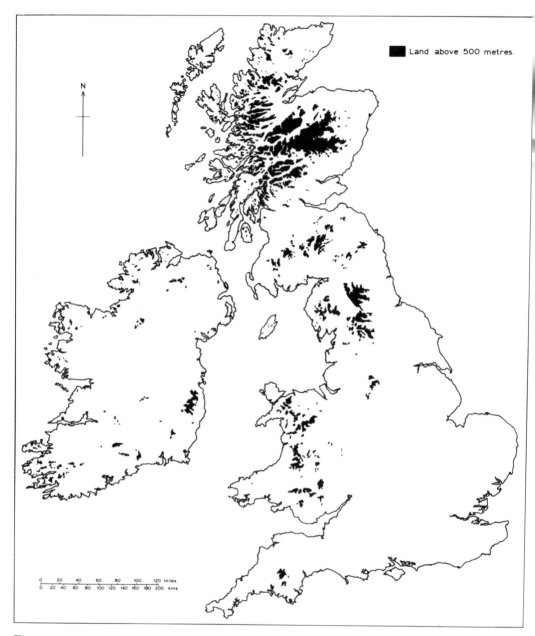

Land above 500 metres.

N

0 20 40 60 80 100 120 Miles.
0 20 40 60 80 100 120 140 160 180 200 Kms.

Fig. 1.

into two distinct regions. The one in the north and west, with all the mountains in it, is the highland region (though it includes some lowland areas). The smaller part in the south-east is the lowland region (though it has a few ranges of hills such as the Malverns, the Chilterns, the Cotswolds and the North and South Downs). Though Ireland has some fine uplands it is largely a lowland country whose natural history is much influenced by its closeness to the Atlantic. But because so many Irish plants and animals are the same as those of Scotland, northern England and Wales, it is usual for naturalists to think of Ireland as part of the highland region of the British Isles. This distinction also holds good for geographers: in the highland region (including Ireland) there is a great predominance of very old rocks while the lowland region is almost entirely an area of younger rocks.

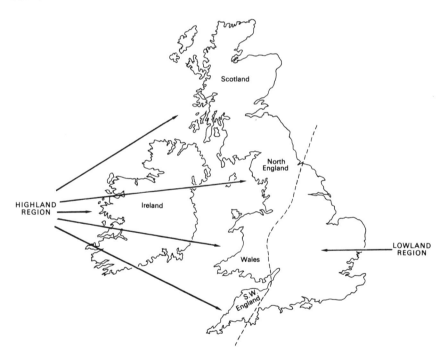

Fig. 2. Highland and lowland regions of the British Isles.

In this book we shall be looking only at the highland region. But don't despair if you live far from mountain country and can hardly ever get there. For some of the things we shall find out about mountains will be true of the hills of lowland Britain as well. Even on the smallest hills there are discoveries to be made and problems to be solved.

2. What is a Mountain?

How did mountains get there in the first place? By studying them all over the world, geologists have discovered four common ways in which they have been formed.

1. By pressure. The rocks have been forced up into a bulge or fold by pressures travelling through the earth's crust. At first many of the rocks were in level layers because they were originally deposits (sediments) of mud, silt and stones lying on the beds of former oceans. These deposits became so thick that eventually they hardened into rock. The rocks that are formed in this way are called sedimentary rocks.

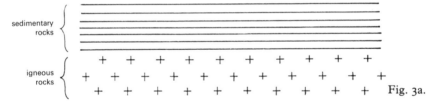

Fig. 3a.

Then pressure caused by very slow but enormously strong movements in the crust made them arch up to form mountains like this:

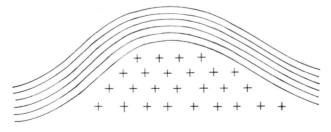

Fig. 3b.

You can imitate this way of forming a mountain by placing your hands on a table-cloth and moving them towards each other, causing the cloth to buckle into an upward fold. Geologists call such a fold in rocks an anticline. Some of the world's greatest mountain ranges have been caused by folding of this sort: in Europe, the Pyrenees and the Alps; in Asia, the Caucasus and the Himalayas; in Africa, the Atlas; in America, the Rockies and the Andes. The upfolding of some mountain ranges continues to this day. Scientists report, for instance, that the Alps are still getting higher—at the rate of 1 mm every year. The Alps, Pyrenees, Himalayas and others are huge folds. But you will find plenty of examples of little folds for yourself if you look at some of the rocks exposed in quarries, sea cliffs or mountain precipices.

2. The second way in which mountains have been formed is by volcanoes. Here and there inside the earth's crust lie rocks that are under such especially great pressure that they are immensely hot, so hot in fact that they have melted. These underground melted (or molten) rocks are known as magma. In a volcanic eruption this magma is forced up through weak spots in the earth's crust and it either flows out on to the surface in the form of lava or it explodes into the air as liquid or solid particles. After the eruption these materials soon cool down and solidify into rocks. Then, if more eruptions follow, these rocks may build up into a very high peak. (Fig. 4.)

Throughout the world there are or have been large numbers of volcanoes. Most have been extinct for many thousands or millions of years but about 450 have erupted in the past 2,000 years. In Europe the best known active ones are Vesuvius in Italy and Etna in Sicily. The nearest active volcanoes to Britain are in Iceland. There are also many places in the world where, although no volcanoes now exist, there are plenty of volcanic rocks to show that volcanoes certainly were there long ago. In the highland zone of Britain there are a great many remains of such ancient volcanoes and though they have been extinct for millions of years they still affect our lives because of the volcanic soils they have left behind.

3. The third common way in which mountains have been formed is by faulting. A fault is a crack in the earth's rocks. It may be only a tiny

Fig. 4.

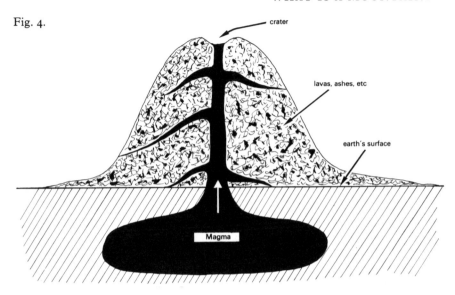

fissure; but some faults are huge, stretching for vast distances across country and deeply underground as well. Sometimes the tension that causes these splits in the earth's crust has been so immense that one side of the fault has been pushed up high enough above the other to form a range of mountains.

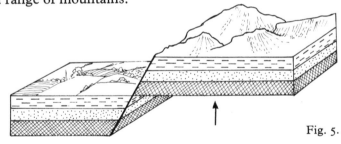

Fig. 5.

4. The fourth way in which mountain peaks have been formed is by being carved out of a more or less flat-topped block of high ground called a plateau. When we want to carve a piece of wood we get a sharp knife and little by little we cut the wood to the shape we want. It's a slow job if the wood is very hard but quicker if the wood is soft. Though mountains are not carved by knives they are shaped by forces

19

that are just as effective, such as rain, wind, sun and frost. All these are hard at work year after year, century after century. This wearing away of the mountains by the elements is called weathering or, more usually, erosion.

A plateau may start like this—a level stretch of high land:

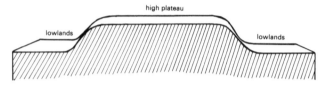

Fig. 6a.

But under the attack of the weather it gradually gets worn down. If its rock is of the same hardness all through it will wear away (erode) evenly and after millions of years may look like this:

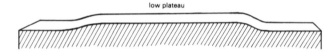

Fig. 6b.

But suppose the plateau is a mixture of hard and soft rocks like this:

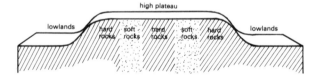

Fig. 6c.

In this plateau the soft rocks may wear entirely away, leaving the hard rocks standing up as peaks:

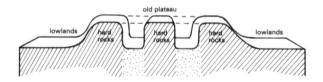

Fig. 6d.

If you climb the Cairngorm Mountains in Scotland you will see that this is what has happened to them. Erosion has carved huge hollows between the mountains; and the mountains themselves instead of being sharp peaks still have the flat tops that were part of the ancient plateau. The Cairngorms are only one example of many such carved up plateaus (or plateaux if you prefer to spell it the French way). You will discover plenty of other examples as you explore elsewhere in Britain.

Perhaps the most obvious difference between the lowlands and the uplands is that whereas the rocks of the lowlands are mostly well buried under soil, those of the uplands outcrop in nearly every view. Yet even in the uplands there is at least a thin covering of soil over most of the surface. Without soils there would be no vegetation except those lichens, mosses and liverworts which can cling to bare rock. So soil is enormously important and we should ask ourselves where it originates. The answer is that it comes from the wearing away of the rocks. The slow but unceasing forces of erosion gradually reduce the rock to particles which form the mountain soils, particles that contain the chemicals of the original rocks. So different sorts of rocks produce different kinds of soils which in their turn support different species of plants (the flora) and animals (the fauna).

A type of erosion that is not at all obvious is that caused by lichens. These strange plants, each a union of an alga with a fungus, are the world's hardiest plants, growing on bare, exposed rocks even on the summits of very high mountains. As they cling to the rock they help to wear it away by producing acids which eat into the surface of the rock, slowly causing it to crumble and produce the soil needed by other kinds of plants.

Now let us look at the erosion of the rocks by weathering. Take rain, for instance. Rainfall and snowfall are heavy on our mountains; and water is always busily shifting earth, stones and even big rocks downhill. Some water seeps slowly through the soil, moving it particle by particle. But meanwhile other water is rushing down steep gullies, cataracts and falls, gouging out rocks and earth and carrying all this waste matter of the uplands down to lowland rivers and out to sea, where it eventually comes to rest on the ocean bed. Rocks and stones themselves can become forces of erosion: as they are pushed and rolled downhill by the water they rasp and grate against both the bed and the banks of streams and rivers and so help to wear them away.

When you go into mountain country you see proof everywhere of the enormous power that water has. In the course of ages the merest trickle may cut itself a gully many metres deep. Lower down the slopes the trickles flow together to form streamlets that carve even bigger gullies and then the streamlets join to form the rivers that create the major valleys between the mountains. And if it seems to you that all these gullies and valleys are out of all proportion huge compared with the amount of water flowing down them, then think what a long time it has taken to form them. Remember also the floods. If you go to the mountains in a spell of dry weather the streams will look very small and feeble. But after a few hours of heavy rain the streams can suddenly become immensely powerful torrents and then you won't be surprised at what they have accomplished as carvers of the landscape. Note too the changed colour of the water. In dry weather it is sparkling and clear. But when swollen by floods it is brown with the mountain earth it is carting off down to the lowlands.

This sort of erosion by water is obvious enough. But water can also be a hidden agent of erosion. Rain does not fall as pure water. It gathers carbon dioxide and ammonia from the atmosphere and these turn it into an acid capable of dissolving some of the chemicals in the rocks and carrying them away downhill invisibly in solution. So even a sparkling clear stream that doesn't seem to be causing any erosion at all is really still helping to wear the mountains away.

Then there's the wind. On mountains the wind seldom stops blowing and the higher you go the stronger it is likely to be. Sometimes it brings rain but often it has a drying effect. In fine summer weather when the sun is scorching down, any exposed surfaces of rock get hot and expanded. Then in the chill air of night they become cold and contracted. This repeated stretching and contracting gradually loosens the surface of the rock and it breaks up into fragments of stone or grains of dust which are either washed away by rain or blown away by wind. And just as pebbles moving along a stream bed can act as grinding agents, so sand grains hurled along by a gale can help to wear rocks away.

Another important weathering agent is frost. First comes the rain and some of this seeps down into cracks in the rocks. Then the weather turns cold and the water freezes. But water swells as it turns into ice—only slightly but with an irresistible force that makes the crack a little wider. When the thaw comes the ice melts away and perhaps the crack dries up. But in the next rain it fills again with water. Then comes another frost and the ice widens the crack a bit more. And so it goes on until at last the crack gets so wide that a piece of rock is broken from the main face and falls.

Fig. 7.

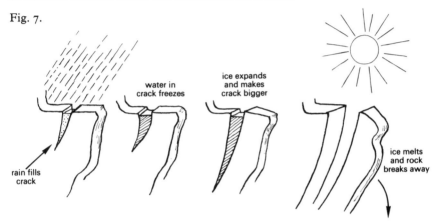

This process of thawing and freezing, repeated many times a year for a vast period of time, has helped to create great precipices on some of our mountains and left the slopes below covered with a scatter of broken rock we call scree.

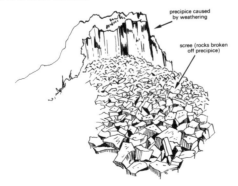

Fig. 8.

23

Such precipices are especially common on the north and east sides of our mountains because these are the frostiest places, being out of the sun and away from the mild south-west winds.

One mighty shaper of our British uplands is no longer at work. I mean the deep layers of slowly creeping ice called glaciers which, until about ten thousand years ago, had covered most of the country for about a million years. These immensely heavy glaciers—in places they reached hundreds of metres thick (as they still do in Greenland and Antarctica)—were the result of falls of snow piling up one upon the other, century after century, and hardening into ice.

As they made their way downhill (by force of gravity) the glaciers gathered a mixture of earth and rock that got frozen into their undersides. Think what irresistible power a huge moving ice-sheet must have as it bites into the earth, armed with rocks as sharp as teeth. This was erosion on a really huge scale and some of the effects on the landscape were sensational.

Take corries, for example. You won't go far in mountain country before you discover a corrie. Perhaps you are making your way

1. Cliffs and screes being colonised by woodland

24

upwards by following the steep course of a torrent. As you climb you find the valley getting narrower, the slopes on either side steeper and higher. Then you come up at last to the place where your stream is born: it flows out of a dark, deep-looking, rock-circled lake. It's a lake that lies in the bottom of a huge, bowl-like hollow with great crags standing round in a semi-circle. This immense hollow in the mountainside has been mainly scooped out by glaciers scraping their way down from some majestic ice-cap. This great basin is a corrie. Another name for it is cirque. Corrie is Scottish, cirque is French. In Welsh the word *cwm* often means a corrie (as in Cwm Idwal) but *cwm* is also a general word for valley. The English language has no word for corrie at all and so has borrowed 'corrie' and 'cirque'.

On some mountains corries have developed opposite to each other and this has led to the formation of knife-edge ridges. First the corries were far apart, as in this view from above:

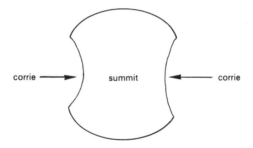

Fig. 9a.

Then by erosion they bit deeper into the mountain's flanks, producing a narrow ridge:

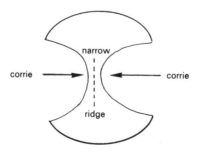

Fig. 9b.

25

And finally a knife edge is formed:

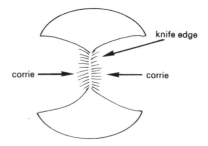

Fig. 9c.

Sometimes several corries have formed to produce not a knife edge but a Matterhorn-like sharp, rocky peak:

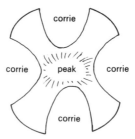

Fig. 9d.

Snowdon is such a peak.

As the great, slow rivers of ice flowed steeply down through the corries to the valleys below, they collected piles of soil and rocks that had fallen from the shattered cliffs and they brought them along as well. The valleys, before the Ice Age, had been worn by rivers and were gorge-like and rocky, and roughly shaped like a V. But the glaciers, armed with their rocks, scoured them out, smoothed their sides and shaped them into a U.

Let us think for a minute about the very end of the Ice Age, the time when the climate again grew mild and the glaciers disappeared from Britain. After the ice-sheets what was left behind? There was a lot of water from the melted ice and there was the earth and rock that had been frozen into the ice. Most of the water hastened away down the rivers to the sea. But some couldn't escape because its path was blocked by the earth and rock which the glaciers deposited. So lakes

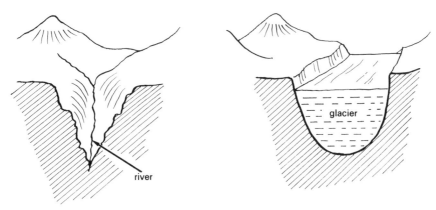

Fig. 10. (*left*) V-shaped valley carved by a river before the Ice Age; (*right*) The same valley smoothed into a U-shape by a glacier

2. A mountain lake dammed behind a glacial moraine

were formed behind natural dams and also in glacier-scooped hollows. And though many lakes have disappeared in the course of ten thousand years there are hundreds still to be seen. We have a special name for the earth and rock left when glaciers have melted. It is moraine. In exploring the uplands you will come upon lots of moraines. But not every pile of rock is a moraine. You should get some expert to show you a genuine moraine first. Then, when you know what you are looking for, go off and seek others for yourself.

Something else you can look out for are rock faces that have been worn flat by glaciers. They are common on our mountains and on some of them you can still see the scratches that were clawed into them by other rocks moving with the ice-sheets. Here again you need to be careful that you really are finding ice scratches, because there are often grooves on rock surfaces that have been caused by other means. So a little tuition from someone in the field will save you from mistakes. These scratches are precious clues. They tell us which way the glacier was moving (ice does not always travel downhill: pressure from other glaciers can force it uphill); and they tell us how high up the mountainside the glacier reached.

Sometimes, perhaps in the middle of flat moorlands, you will come upon a huge boulder lying on the surface. Naturally you wonder how it got there, for there are no cliffs anywhere near that it could have fallen from and it is far too huge for anybody to have carried it there. It is, in fact, yet another product of the Ice Age. The rock, eroded from a crag, fell crashing on to a moving ice-sheet and was slowly transported far from where it started. Then the great thaw arrived, the glacier melted and left the rock lying on the moorland. Rocks transported and then dumped by glaciers are called erratic boulders (erratic means wandering). They were a puzzle to past generations, who usually 'explained' them by fanciful stories that they had been thrown around by giants. It wasn't until the middle of the nineteenth century that the truth about these displaced boulders was discovered.

One of the least spectacular effects of Ice Age erosion is perhaps the most important of all—soil spreading. Over most of the British Isles the soil is largely made up of the materials that thawed out of the great depths of ice that covered the land (except England south of the

3.
An erratic
boulder
deposited
by the melting
of a glacier

Thames, which the ice-sheets never reached). And since the ice-sheets were always on the move the soils they left behind had come, like the erratic boulders, from somewhere else. These soils, usually called transported soils or drift soils, are often very fertile because on their journeys in the glaciers they collected minerals from many different rocks. Some of the best farming land is made of drift soils. Boulder clay is a typical drift soil. It covers great areas both of highland and lowland Britain and is so called because of the stones it contains, stones that vary in size from small pebbles to very big rocks. You can see the sort of stuff boulder clay is when it is exposed in clay pits, river banks or sea cliffs. It looks like this:

Fig. 11. Boulder clay

29

You may wonder how we can be sure that soil spreading really happened in this way (and you are quite right to doubt all theories until they are proved correct). If you visit a part of the world where glaciers still exist (the Alps, for instance) you will see them at work, plucking rocks out of the cliffs, carrying stones and soil and leaving moraines and erratic boulders down the valleys. It was in the Alps that glaciation began to be studied in the first half of last century by Louis Agassiz, a Swiss naturalist. He later visited Britain and was the first man to point out that great masses of ice had once covered much of the British Isles. His evidence was the moraines, the scratched rocks, the erratic blocks which he found in abundance all over highland Britain. Everybody knew they were there but he knew what they were because he had studied them in the Alps.

In other words he was a good detective. And a good detective is what you must become if you are going to understand about nature and how it works.

3. The World Changes as you Climb

In this chapter we shall look quickly at the different belts of vegetation (naturalists call them zones) that you can expect to pass through as you climb a mountain. Then in other chapters we can take a closer look at these zones.

The English names of plants and animals can be misleading, so throughout this book, whenever a plant or animal is first mentioned, its scientific name will be given afterwards in brackets.

Most mountain climbs begin in a valley among farms, fields and hedges. Here the animals, birds, insects and plants are the sorts you would expect to find almost anywhere in lowland country. Typical trees are oak (*Quercus petraea*) and ash (*Fraxinus excelsior*), the most obvious wild mammals are rabbits (*Oryctolagus cuniculus*) and squirrels (grey ones—*Sciurus carolinensis*—in many districts but also red ones—*Sciurus vulgaris*); the commonest birds are finches, thrushes, warblers, starlings (*Sturnus vulgaris*), woodpigeons (*Columba palumbus*) and crows. Perhaps it is a fine summer day with plenty of butterflies about—meadow browns (*Maniola jurtina*), speckled woods (*Pararge aegeria*), gatekeepers (*Maniola tithonus*), walls (*Pararge megera*), peacocks (*Nymphalis io*) and small tortoise-shells (*Aglais urticae*); many of the fields are level and growing corn or are pastures full of sleek cattle. Such is the lowland valley zone, where life is sheltered and warm and soils are deep and fertile.

Then you go up the first slopes. And in many places you soon find yourself in steep woodland, possibly a mixture of oak, ash and birch (*Betula* spp.). You will quickly spot a big difference between this kind of woodland and the sort you usually find in the lowlands: it has

4. An unfenced high-level wood of scrub oak (*Quercus petraea*). Note the absence of undergrowth because of grazing.

scarcely any undergrowth in it compared with a lowland oakwood with its dense understorey of hazel (*Corylus avellana*), hawthorn (*Crataegus monogyna*), holly (*Ilex aquifolium*) and other bushes and small trees. Why this difference? It is simply that the hillside woods are usually unfenced, which means they are grazed in by sheep and often cattle, ponies and, in some districts, deer as well. These animals can come down the slopes into the woods any time they need shelter from bad weather or shade on hot days. By their grazing they prevent all undergrowth and young trees from developing and they destroy most of the wild flowers.

Oakwoods don't stretch very far up the slopes. Maybe when you are still at less than 300 m (985 ft) above sea level you reach the tree line (or tree limit). Above that the going may be easy over short turf; or you may have to battle through a zone of bracken (*Pteridium aquilinum*) which grows very thickly on some slopes up to maybe

500 m (1640 ft). But then you reach a height where the bracken thins out and soon you leave it behind altogether. In the Scottish Highlands the tree line is higher because there, above the oakwoods, you will often come up into a belt of birch and pine, which are hardier trees than oak.

Not many British mountains go steeply up all the way like the slope of a roof. The going may be severe at first, then it eases, then it's steep again, then easier and so it changes all the way to the top. The steepest places are usually the driest because the rainwater runs off them quickly. But where the ground is nearly level it can be boggy underfoot even in summer.

Though there's no shortage of bogs on our uplands there are vast areas of good firm grassland too, climbing away towards the summits. Man has used this grassland zone as cattle ranges and sheepwalks for many hundreds of years and it is only in this century he has found another major use for it—forestry. Since World War I wide areas of the uplands have been covered with conifer plantations and these now form a separate zone with its own special wildlife. You will find the conifer forests reaching up no higher than about 400 m (1310 ft), at least on the exposed western sides of our uplands. Above that you come out to open grasslands again. Or the ground may be covered for great distances by a zone of heather. Or if it is especially wet it may be another stretch of bog. And winding through all this land of grass, bog and planted forests are the many streams that rise in the mountains and flow into and out of lakes which lie in hollows between the ridges.

Eventually you come to the last slope of the mountain. The land gets steeper and rockier. Now you are above the zone of tall heather and have reached one covered by grass, bilberry (*Vaccinium myrtillus*), crowberry (*Empetrum nigrum*) and similar dwarf shrubs. If you are faced with the crags of a corrie it may take you some time to find a way round them. But you manage it at last, you get above the corrie cliffs and are soon at the top of the mountain. This summit zone may be a single peak or a long rocky ridge or simply a flat top (the remains of an ancient plateau) scattered with stones or sometimes huge slabs of loose rock. It will certainly be a bare-looking place with

33

5. A mountain summit. There is an absence of trees and shrubs because only dwarf vegetation can survive in the high winds of such exposed places.

little or no sign of animals, birds or insects, and very scanty vegetation. It is also sure to be a splendid viewpoint. From up there, if the day is clear, you will look down into deep valleys and across to other mountains. And you will learn much about the wearing away of the earth's surface. For this summit and its neighbouring peaks only stand up today because they are made of especially hard rock. The softer rocks which once connected all these peaks into one great plateau have long since been broken up and carried away by the forces of erosion.

So, having climbed our mountain to get a quick glance at its different zones, we can now start at the bottom again and look at them in more detail.

4. Natural Woodland and Bracken

In looking at woodlands let us think first about oaks, for it is oakwoods that you will find on the lowest slopes of many a mountain, small oakwoods that remind us of the vast forests of oak and other trees that once covered not only most of the lowlands but also the uplands to about 600 m (1970 ft).

There are two kinds of oak that are natural (or native) in the British Isles: the sessile oak (*Quercus petraea*) and the pedunculate oak (*Quercus robur*), and it is worth knowing how to distinguish them. Both are widespread but in highland Britain it is the sessile oak that is commoner. So much so that in many a mountainside wood the sessile oak is the only oak present.

This you can most easily test for yourself when the acorns are on the trees from August to October because it is by their acorns that you will best identify the two oak species. Perhaps your idea of an acorn is that the cup it fits into is fixed to a stalk like this:

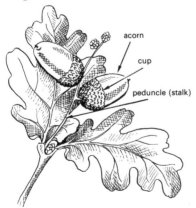

Fig. 12a.

If so you are evidently most familiar with pedunculate oaks, for that is how their acorns are arranged: their cups are at the end of little stalks called peduncles.

But in a mountainside oakwood you are more likely to find that the acorn cups do not have stalks. Instead they sit directly on the twigs among the leaves like this:

Fig. 12b.

It is these oaks whose acorns sit directly on the twigs that are the sessile oaks (sessile means sitting).

Sessile oak is a hardy and adaptable tree. You soon realise this when you see what rocky, thin, infertile soil it often grows in. It flourishes in conditions in which trees such as pedunculate oak, ash, wych elm (*Ulmus glabra*), beech (*Fagus sylvatica*) and lime (*Tilia* spp.) are not often found unless they have been planted by man.

Looking back into pre-history, when much of the British Isles was covered with forest, we can be pretty sure that most of the lower mountain slopes were covered by sessile oaks. But already in pre-history man was beginning to make clearings with the aid of fire and stone axes. Since then the oak forest has got less and less. Man has felled it to make clearings for his farms; to build ships, houses, bridges; to make charcoal (the main fuel burnt in the furnaces of early industry); and for the manufacture of tannin, a substance extracted from oak bark and used in leather-making. The small hillside oakwoods that still survive are kept to provide the farms with fencing posts and to shelter sheep and cattle from wind, rain and snow in winter.

In most of these unfenced woods where grazing animals prevent the spread of undergrowth you will find little wildlife except up in the trees themselves. Among the branches in spring and summer there are many insects and plenty of birds to feed on them. Many of the birds are hole-nesters, such as tits, flycatchers, redstarts (*Phoenicurus*

6. The pied flycatcher (*Ficedula hypoleuca*) breeds mainly in the oakwoods of Wales and the north of England.

phoenicurus), tree creepers (*Certhia familiaris*), nuthatches (*Sitta europaea*), woodpeckers and starlings. Some build in the branches: buzzard (*Buteo buteo*), crow, mistle thrush (*Turdus viscivorus*), chaffinch (*Fringilla coelebs*); some nest on the ground: robin (*Erithacus rubecula*), tree pipit (*Anthus trivialis*), willow warbler (*Phylloscopus trochilus*) and wood warbler (*Phylloscopus sibilatrix*). But the typical undergrowth-nesters of lowland woods—blackbird (*Turdus merula*), song thrush (*Turdus philomelos*), wren (*Troglodytes troglodytes*), chiffchaff (*Phylloscopus collybita*) and other warblers— have difficulty in finding housing sites in much-grazed woodlands.

In the breeding season most of the woodland birds feed their young on moth caterpillars from the oaks, for no other tree has such a

37

numerous insect population. Three kinds of moth caterpillar are especially abundant on oak leaves both in lowland and hillside woods: those of the winter moth (*Operophtera brumata*), the mottled umber (*Erannis defoliaria*) and the oak tortrix (*Tortrix viridana*). In most years they form an inexhaustible supply of food in June, precisely when woodland birds need vast numbers of caterpillars to feed their young on.

Fig. 13.
Mottled umber moth
(*Erannis defoliaria*):
male (left) and wingless female

Some hillside oakwoods, even though unfenced, are richer in wildlife than others. In boggy woods, for instance, or woods growing on rough bouldery scree where grazing is difficult, there are usually more plant and animal species. A scree of big boulders (block scree) with its many caverns and passages between the boulders can provide refuge for wild cats (*Felis sylvestris*) (in Scotland), polecats (*Mustela putorius*) (in Wales), foxes (*Vulpes vulpes*), stoats (*Mustela erminia*), weasels (*Mustela nivalis*) and pine martens (*Martes martes*). In very damp woods both rocks and trees may be covered by mosses of many kinds and branches often bristle with polypody ferns and bearded lichens. Among the rocks you will usually find tall ferns: lady-fern (*Athyrium filix-femina*), male-fern (*Dryopteris filix-mas*), broad buckler-fern (*Dryopteris dilatata*), lemon-scented fern (*Thelypteris limbosperma*) and hard fern (*Blechnum spicant*).

In a wood where grazing happens to be light or absent you may find bluebells (*Endymion non-scriptus*), primroses (*Primula vulgaris*), wood-sorrel (*Oxalis acetosella*), pignut (*Conopodium majus*), wood anemones (*Anemone nemorosa*), common cow-wheat (*Melampyrum pratense*), foxgloves (*Digitalis purpurea*) and many other wild flowers.

And where grazing and trampling are slight you may even see bluebells on open grassland far from trees: they are a reminder of woodland that grew there perhaps long ago.

In limestone districts of the north of England, especially Yorkshire and Derbyshire, the natural woodland is mainly of ash, because oak and birch do not flourish in limestone soils. In fenced ashwoods there is often a great profusion of wild flowers, both because the soil is fertile and because ash leaves cast only a light shade on the ground. In some upland ashwoods, even where there is no fence, the wild flowers are safe from grazing because they grow down in deep cracks (grikes) which are characteristic of limestone country.

By far the most abundant fern on lower mountain slopes is bracken. If it grows in the shelter of woodland in deep, well-drained soil it may grow taller than a man. Even on windy hillsides outside the woods it will reach a metre or more and cover vast areas with such a dense jungle that it smothers all other plants, even the toughest kinds of grass. Small wonder the hill farmers have no love for it. As you climb higher and conditions get harder the bracken becomes more and more stunted until it may fade out altogether on exposed slopes before you reach 500 m (1640 ft). But on the slopes sheltered from the prevailing winds you will sometimes find bracken reaching to 600 m (1970 ft). Above that it is too frosty for it everywhere. Another enemy of bracken is the hooves of cattle, which break off the young shoots in spring. So where cattle are regularly foraging there is likely to be more grass than bracken. With sheep things are different. Sheep are light-footed, stepping delicately among the bracken fronds. So on sheep pastures the bracken may spread in all directions. Bracken is poisonous to some animals. Sheep and rabbits rarely touch it but cattle are occasionally killed by eating too much of it. Sometimes bracken is recommended as a food for man but modern researchers suspect it can cause serious disease. Some insects, however, thrive on it, one of the easiest to find being the caterpillars of the broom moth (*Ceramica pisi*): they have yellow and brown stripes along the length of their bodies and feed conspicuously by day on bracken in August and September.

Farmers have always longed to get rid of these stretches of bracken

7. Usually chocolate coloured with bold yellow stripes, the caterpillar of the broom moth (*Ceramica pisi*) is conspicuous on bracken in August and September.

that cover such huge areas of semi-upland Britain but till recently the task has seemed too huge. These days they are looking hopefully at selective weed-killers. Spraying the hillsides by helicopter is now the fashion and if these herbicides prove to be an effective long-term method of control then the lower slopes of the hills are destined to look very different from what they are today, especially in autumn and winter, when as the bracken dies down they turn to a rich red-brown which makes them very beautiful. Naturalists point out that bracken, although not rich in wildlife, is certainly a better habitat than sheep-nibbled grassland. It shelters insects and birds and what's more it can act as a protection for young trees such as hawthorn and rowan (*Sorbus aucuparia*). If a seedling tree springs up in a sheep pasture it quickly gets eaten. But if it germinates amid a dense growth of bracken there is a chance that the sheep will not find it. So it may survive to become an adult tree.

A species of tree often abundant among the hillside oaks is the birch. So much so that many woods are better called birch-oakwoods than just oakwoods. Sessile oak is hardy but birch is far hardier, as you can see most clearly in the Scottish Highlands where you will find birchwoods higher up the slopes than oakwoods ever are.

8. Birchwoods (*Betula* spp.) once covered great areas on British mountainsides. Today they survive mainly in Scotland.

Probably, before man cleared away the forests, birch covered great areas of our mountain slopes, especially in Scotland, and was, except for oak, Britain's commonest tree. So it is natural that a large number of insects have become adapted to birchwood life. In spring and summer there are often plenty of caterpillar-eating birds in the upland birchwoods, small birds such as chaffinches, willow warblers, tree pipits, robins, redstarts, and great, long-tailed, coal and blue tits (*Parus major*, *Aegithalos caudatus*, *Parus ater* and *Parus caeruleus*). In autumn and winter the birches yield vast quantities of seeds which are eagerly sought by finches, especially siskins (*Carduelis spinus*) and redpolls (*Acanthis flammea*).

Scots pine too was very common in the first forests to invade Britain immediately after the Ice Age. Then, as the climate went on getting milder, the oaks began to spread into south-east England from the Continent, for in those times there was no sea between Britain and the rest of Europe. Gradually the oak forest advanced west and north, taking the place of pine until all that was left of the ancient pine forest was in the Scottish Highlands, where today it still forms beautiful patches of natural woodland up hillsides here and there to a height of 600 m (1970 ft).

To see Scots pine at its best you should visit Rothiemurchus Forest near Aviemore or some other Highland locality famous for its pines. What chiefly distinguishes forests planted by man from natural forests is that in plantations the trees are all about the same age, whereas in natural forests like the old Scottish pinewoods you find trees of all ages, from seedlings to ancient giants, all growing as neighbours.

Thick carpets of bilberry, heather and crowberry form much of the undergrowth of these old forests. And higher up the slopes you may reach a level where cranberry (*Vaccinium oxycoccus*) and bearberry (*Arctostaphylos uva-ursi*) become the commonest mat-formers. The pines are not crowded together as they are in plantations. If they were you would find no ground vegetation at all because it would be too dark under the trees for plants to grow. Instead the trees are well spaced with plenty of clearings and in these clearings grows a tall evergreen shrub called juniper (*Juniperus communis*), either standing alone or forming small thickets.

Colourful wild flowers are few in these Scottish forests of pine and birch. The yellow tormentil (*Potentilla erecta*) and the fragrant, white heath bedstraw (*Galium saxatile*) are very common, as they are throughout highland Britain. And there are some choice rarities such as one-flowered wintergreen (*Moneses uniflora*); coralroot orchid (*Corallorhiza trifida*); another orchid, creeping lady's tresses (*Goodyera repens*) which has a spiral of little white flowers; lesser twayblade (*Listera cordata*), also an orchid but with small reddish spikes; and, most distinguished, the twinflower, a small creeping plant with two drooping pink flowers and named by science *Linnaea borealis* to commemorate the great Swedish botanist Linnaeus (1707–78) who was a pioneer in giving scientific names to plants and animals.

42

9. The Scots pine (*Pinus sylvestris*) is widespread in the British Isles because man has planted it in large numbers. But it is native only in Scotland, where there are still relics of the ancient forests.

NATURAL WOODLAND AND BRACKEN

The Highland pine forests have their special animals and birds. The red deer (*Cervus elaphus*), which enjoy the upper mountain slopes in summer, are glad to come down among the trees for winter shelter. A smaller deer, the roe (*Capreolus capreolus*), is more of a woodlander at all seasons, though in some parts of Scotland it too lives on treeless uplands. Its loud gruff bark is one of the typical sounds of the pine forest. In July and August, their breeding time (called the rutting season), the male roe deer fight a great deal.

A mammal of the weasel family which from its name you might expect to be common in these Scottish pine forests is the pine marten. But these days the marten is no longer numerous anywhere in Britain. It survives as an extreme rarity in some wilder parts of Wales, the Lake District and Ireland, and even in the old pinewoods of Scotland it is far from common. If you can manage a visit to the Beinn Eighe National Nature Reserve in the North-West Highlands, you will find a most enjoyable nature trail climbing up the mountainside from the shores of Loch Maree. This is the sort of place, among rocks, heather and great old pines, where you might find traces of a marten or even be lucky enough to see one. For although mostly nocturnal, martens sometimes come out by day in quiet places. Martens are extremely agile, able to climb trees and leap about the branches like squirrels. In fact they sometimes prey on squirrels. And if a marten catches a squirrel in the old Scottish pinewoods it will be a red squirrel. For the grey squirrel, which is a foreign species introduced to England from America in the late nineteenth century, has not yet spread as far north as the Scottish Highlands. So the red squirrel, which has disappeared from many parts of southern Britain as the grey squirrel has advanced, still flourishes in the pinewoods of the north.

Among typical breeding birds of Scottish pinewoods are siskin, goldcrest (*Regulus regulus*), tree pipit, redstart, willow warbler and wood warbler. But there are many others, including three that are local or rare: crossbill (*Loxia curvirostra*), crested tit (*Parus cristatus*) and capercaillie (*Tetrao urogallus*). Remember when you are looking for crossbills that they often feed very high up in the great pines, prising open the cones to get at the seeds. They may be quite silent as

44

Fig. 14.
(*above*) Red deer
(*Cervus elaphus*);
(*left*) roe deer
(*Capreolus capreolus*)

they feed and your best hope of spotting them is when they fly from one tree to another making their sharp *chip-chip-chip* calls. The soft churring note of crested tits is equally distinctive, but you need to listen for it carefully because they too may feed high in the pines, where they seek insects rather than seeds.

Fig. 15. Crested tit (*Parus cristatus*)

As for the capercaillie, this is an outsize, black-looking game bird that bursts out of cover with much noise and flapping and then flies strongly away through the trees. You may see capercaillies on the ground or high in trees where they eat shoots of pine or other conifers. They also roost up there at night.

Capercaillie, crested tit and crossbill are not restricted to natural pine forest. They flourish also in the man-made woodlands which are so extensive in modern Britain that they are worth a chapter of their own.

5. Planted Conifers

In the last chapter we finished up in the natural pinewoods of Scotland. They are very wild and beautiful but the area they cover is nothing compared with the plantations of pines, spruces and other conifers now covering many parts of highland Britain. Compared with the thousands of years the Scottish pine forests have endured, the upland plantations are something new. Most of them have been created, by orders of the Government, since about 1920.

Because nearly all our natural forests were cut down centuries ago to make room for farming, Britain has long had to import vast amounts of softwood timber (as the wood from conifers is called) from North America and northern Europe. But after World War I the Government decided we ought to have forests of our own and so the Forestry Commission was created and given the task of planting millions of trees. But where to put them? They couldn't be planted in the fertile ground of the lowlands because that was too valuable as agricultural land. The only place available for big-scale forestry was the sheep-rearing country of the uplands. Mountain farms were bought one after another, the sheep were taken away and fenced out and the little trees were planted, nearly all conifers. The plantations are not on the very highest ground because up there the conditions, especially the winds, are too severe for trees. So plantations even on the sheltered sides of Britain's mountains do not normally reach higher than about 600 m (1970 ft).

From a distance these conifers, because of their dark-green leaves (needles), can look almost black in contrast with the pale grass of nearby hills. The tree most commonly grown is a native of the

47

10. Old mountain grasslands and recently planted conifers. The introduction of trees brings big changes in the ecology of the uplands.

western side of North America, the Sitka spruce (*Picea sitchensis*). Of all the species tried this is the one that seems most suited to grow on ground that is poor, wet and peaty and where the rainfall is great, the winds are strong and frosts in late spring (when the young leaves are sprouting) are frequent.

But not all the uplands are ill-drained, peaty and exposed. There are drier slopes with deeper soils, rocky places with thin soils; valleys which though high are nicely sheltered; and many other different habitats. In these other sites different conifers are used. Larch (*Larix* sp.), for instance, and Scots pine (*Pinus sylvestris*); Norway spruce (*Picea abies*), which is familiar to us all as the Christmas tree;

48

lodgepole pine (*Pinus contorta*), formerly used as wigwam posts by North American Indians; western hemlock (*Tsuga heterophylla*), Douglas fir (*Pseudotsuga menziesii*), grand fir (*Abies grandis*), noble fir (*Abies procera*), Western red cedar (*Thuja plicata*) and a few others. None of them, except Scots pine, is a British native species.

What about the wildlife in these plantations of conifers? If you change open country into forest you are obviously going to alter the whole natural history of the place. Let us think first of all about the birds, because they are the easiest to observe. The effects on birds may begin faster than you might expect. In fact, just putting up a row of fencing stakes across a stretch of rushy moorland can be enough to persuade whinchats (*Saxicola rubetra*) to breed there. This is because the male whinchats—they select the nesting territory—like to have tall perches which they can use as singing places and look-out posts.

When the fence has been completed no more sheep, cattle, ponies or deer can get in. Just think what an event this is. Maybe for the first time in a thousand years the moorland plants can develop properly, safe at last from the nibbling teeth (incisors) of all those large animals. The new growth can be quite dramatic in only a few months. Outside the fence the vegetation is still cropped very short: a habitat that is attractive to few upland birds except wheatears (*Oenanthe oenanthe*). Inside the fence there is beginning to develop a wilderness of grasses, heather, bilberry, crowberry, gorse (*Ulex* sp.) and other plants as well as the little conifers. In this thick cover there are more birds—notably more meadow pipits (*Anthus pratensis*), cuckoos (*Cuculus canorus*), skylarks (*Alauda arvensis*) and whinchats—than there are outside the forest fence.

As well as these small birds there is usually a big increase in the populations of small rodents and shrews which love this new world of long grass and other plants which provide them with generous supplies of food and shelter. Field voles (*Microtus agrestis*) especially may multiply exceedingly and when this happens they become an attraction for exceptional numbers of predators such as kestrels (*Falco tinnunculus*), buzzards, short-eared owls (*Asio flammeus*) and foxes. Very occasionally there have been real plagues when the voles have eaten the grass down to the bare earth and also killed many

11. Nest of a short-eared owl (*Asio flammeus*) under a young spruce. Owls are among several predators, both birds and mammals, attracted by the voles abundant in young plantations.

young conifers by nibbling at the bark. Eventually starvation and over-crowding have brought mass disease and the population has dropped suddenly from multitudinous to sparse.

Fig. 16. Field vole (*Microtus agrestis*)

Let us allow a few years to go by after the first planting of the forest. The little trees reach a height of a couple of metres and begin to bush out. What happens to the birds now? If you visit such a plantation in May or June you will find that quite a number of bush-nesting species have come to breed in the little trees or in the surrounding vegetation. There may be blackbirds, thrushes, bullfinches (*Pyrrhula pyrrhula*), chaffinches, redpolls, linnets (*Acanthis cannabina*), whitethroats (*Sylvia communis*), wrens and hedge-sparrows (*Prunella modularis*); and on the ground below probably robins, yellowhammers (*Emberiza citrinella*) and willow warblers. And in many forests a game-bird called the black grouse (*Lyrurus tetrix*) which lives on conifer shoots. But birds that dislike such thick cover will by now have left. No more meadow pipits, whinchats, skylarks or short-eared owls. They will have gone off to look for younger plantations where the cover is thinner.

Fig. 17. Blackcock (male of black grouse, *Lyrurus tetrix*)

Meanwhile our forest doesn't stay rich in birds for very long. Young trees grow fast and in another couple of years they spread into an impenetrable jungle that stifles all other vegetation by shutting out the light. This killing of the undergrowth robs the birds of a lot of their food supplies, because though they may nest in the spruces they feed mainly on insects, seeds and fruit which they find on grasses, bilberry, heather, gorse and other plants. So one by one the birds cease to breed in these thickening forests. Those that remain tend to live near the edges of the plantations or along the rides and fire-breaks. So the heart of the forest gets ever darker and more silent as the trees grow up and up.

As the spruces become tall the lower branches are lopped off and some of the trees are cut down to give more space to the rest. You can now walk easily all through the forest, the bushy stage is over and it is the turn mainly of the larger birds—woodpigeon, jay (*Garrulus glandarius*), magpie (*Pica pica*) and carrion crow (*Corvus corone corone*). Of small birds only two are plentiful in these taller conifers—coal tit and goldcrest—for both are independent of undergrowth, finding their tiny insect food high in the trees. For a breeding site the goldcrest often hangs her cradle of a nest under the end of a conifer branch; and the coal tit is usually content with just a hole in the ground near the foot of a tree.

The years go by and the forest continues to change. The trees are thinned and thinned again, leaving the best to become the final crop. Now you walk between tall, bare, thick trunks on a deep carpet of needles. The foliage of the trees (called the canopy) is now many metres above your head and the cries of goldcrests and coal tits are faint sounds from invisible birds in the tree tops. It is at this late stage of the forest that a few birds of prey such as sparrowhawk (*Accipiter nisus*), kestrel and buzzard may take up residence. And also two small birds, siskin and crossbill, which breed mainly in Scotland and Ireland but are found increasingly these days nesting in other parts of Britain. In the Scottish Highlands the crested tit begins to breed in conifer plantations at this nearly mature stage. In some districts, especially in Ireland, the long-eared owl (*Asio otus*) is attracted to these older conifers.

At last, after forty, fifty or more years the plantation is cut down. Young trees are planted in its place and the cycle of change begins all over again. I have written only of the birds. But a similar story could be told about the insects; and also about the small mammals. They are abundant in the early stages of the plantations but get fewer and fewer as the trees grow tall: then comes the turn of the larger mammals—foxes, badgers (*Meles meles*), deer and others.

A lot of argument goes on about conifer plantations. As scenery many people find them dismal, monotonous and very unnatural—not nearly as refreshing to the spirit as open moorlands with their greater range of colours and shapes. 'Depressing blankets' is the sort of description these people give to the plantations. The opposition to forestry has been so strong, especially in National Parks, that the Forestry Commission has agreed not to plant trees in certain particularly beautiful areas. The forests are also criticised as obstructions because before they came there was the freedom of the hills for rambling across, whereas now you may be stopped by a forest fence and millions of prickly young spruces.

Another objection is that when you get inside a plantation you find yourself in a shadowy, silent world where there's hardly anything to see except rows and rows of tree trunks, where there are very few wild flowers and where wildlife is very hard to find, if it exists at all. For even a plantation at the bushy stage is lively with birds only in the nesting season: in autumn and winter it can be very birdless.

Some naturalists are particularly sad when, as quite often happens, they see a broad-leaved wood such as an oakwood cut down to make way for conifers, because broad-leaved woods are so much richer in wildlife than conifer woods ever are. The draining of bogs and marshes for forestry has also meant the destruction of valued habitats of animals, birds and plants. Another frequent criticism concerns our food supplies. In these days of expensive meat, say the critics, the uplands would be better employed raising sheep rather than trees.

On the other side of the argument are those who think the conifer plantations are an improvement in the landscape, bringing variety to otherwise monotonous moorlands. They point out that in contrast with the dark-green of the spruces there are the beautiful deciduous larches which are bright-green in spring, golden-yellow in autumn and have attractive red-brown twigs in winter when the leaves have fallen. What's more, the plantations are not entirely conifers: there are small numbers of broad-leaved trees which add variety to the scene.

53

The supporters of forestry admit that years ago some of the plantations were ugly because laid out with unnatural-looking straight edges. But they claim that these days the forests are more carefully shaped to fit into the rolling landscape of the uplands.

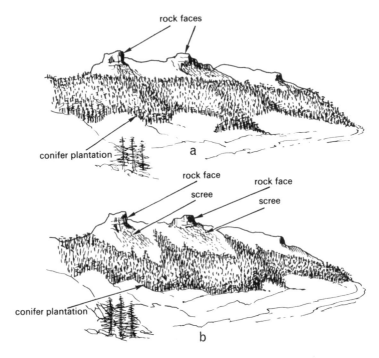

Fig. 18. Bad and good afforestation: in (a) the top edge of the plantation is straight and unnatural; in (b) it has been made to fit in with the shape of the hillside and so looks more like natural forest

Another argument that is made in support of the conifer plantations is that they improve the upland soils. For very many centuries, ever since the hill country lost the protective cover of the primeval forest, the soil has been attacked by leaching, a process by which mineral salts essential to plant life are washed out of the upper layers of soil by percolating rain water and taken down to lower levels where they are beyond the reach of small plants such as grasses. But

54

when trees are planted on the moorlands, so the argument goes, their roots go deep enough into the soil to reach these leached minerals and use them to make trunks, branches and leaves. These leaves eventually fall to the ground to form leaf mould and so a forest soil is created. In this way, foresters claim, fertility is restored to the uplands whereas sheep farming, they say, has for centuries been depriving the soil of minerals in the form of sheep meat, bones and wool and putting very little back, apart from sheep droppings, to make good the losses. Some have objected to this argument by questioning whether the soils created by the conifer plantations are really fertile. Others go so far as to suggest that these soils contain injurious substances which, when washed by rainfall into rivers, can reduce the populations of fish.

There are some naturalists who are in favour of the plantations because while they agree that conifers are not nearly as good for wildlife as broad-leaved woodland is, yet a conifer plantation is probably richer than most stretches of moorland. These naturalists point out what good habitats the very young plantations are for birds and insects. They also claim that the older forests are valuable refuges for animals such as deer, badger and fox and for rarer creatures like wild cat, pine marten, polecat and red squirrel.

The economic argument in favour of forestry is that by providing home-grown timber it saves Britain from having to buy so much wood and wood products (such as paper) from abroad. In other words it helps the country's balance of payments. Forestry also claims to provide more employment than sheep farming does.

One good thing about the upland forests is that in recent years the Forestry Commission has become much more inclined than formerly to welcome the public into the plantations. There have long been a small number of camp sites and picnic areas but now more of these are being developed, as well as car parks, holiday houses, nature trails and interpretation centres.

If you live near or can visit the Lake District you should go to Grizedale, which is between two lakes called Coniston and Estwaite Water. There the Forestry Commission has made a special effort to encourage people to walk the forest roads and observe the forest wild life. You can see several contrasting types of country, from farming land in the valley bottom, up through ancient oakwoods and modern larch plantations, to spruce forest higher still: so you can compare one habitat with another all in one valley. There are nature trails and hides as well as a museum and a nature centre where you can get information about wildlife and forestry. Grizedale is especially known for its deer, both red and roe, and these you may be lucky enough to see from observation towers overlooking clearings in the forest. Let us hope that the sort of wildlife-watching facilities Grizedale offers today will soon become available in state forests throughout Britain. A very interesting booklet about nature and conifer forests is *Wildlife Conservation in Woodlands* by R. C. Steele. This is Forestry Commission Booklet 29.

6. The Mountain Grasslands

When you see the extent of the mountain grasslands (also known as rough hill grazings or upland sheepwalks) you might well suppose that every kind of British grass must grow there. But this would be quite a wrong idea. The truth is that out of the 150 or so species of grass recorded in the British Isles only a handful are at all common on high ground. Life on the hills is full of problems caused by strong winds, heavy rain and snow, long winters, treacherous springs, lack

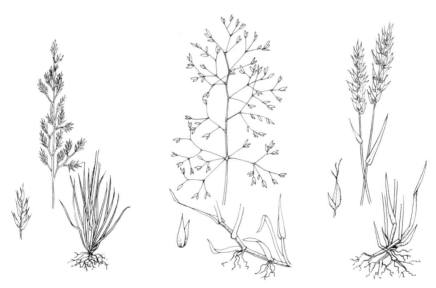

Fig. 19a. (*left*) Sheep's fescue (*Festuca ovina*); b. (*centre*) Common bent (*Agrostis tenuis*); c. (*right*) Sweet vernal-grass (*Anthoxanthum odoratum*)

of sunshine and infertile soils. Only a few grasses have solved all these problems and it is these half-dozen or so that you will find almost wherever you go. One of the most abundant is called sheep's fescue (*Festuca ovina*), which, as the name indicates, is a valuable fodder plant. Often growing with it is a grass called common bent (*Agrostis tenuis*) which is also much eaten by sheep. A third very edible species is sweet vernal-grass (*Anthoxanthum odoratum*): its leaves have a delicate scent in early spring, enough to make the air slightly fragrant.

When you have learned to identify these three grasses you will find many a well-drained hillside where they are easily the commonest plants. Super-abundant species like these are what are known as dominant. But though these species are so successful at keeping their rivals out, there are a few other plants which are common in this type of mountain turf, among them tormentil, heath bedstraw, heath milkwort (*Polygala serpyllifolia*), sheep's sorrel (*Rumex acetosella*), heath speedwell (*Veronica officinalis*) and several mosses. In some upland regions the yellow (or sometimes violet) mountain pansy (*Viola lutea*) brings a touch of colour to the grasslands.

Wherever you go in the grassy hills in summer there are likely to be sheep not far away. Don't ignore them just because they are domestic animals. For no matter what particular branch of nature study you are interested in, the grazing of sheep is an important influence on the habitat and there are lessons to be learned from it. If you get to know a mountain really well you will very likely notice that the sheep feed much more often in some places than others. Now if you have a close look at one of these sheep-favoured slopes you will probably find it occupied by fescue and common bent. But what about the nearby hillside which the sheep seem careful to avoid? Examine it carefully and you may well find it is covered not by fescue or bent but by a wiry species called mat-grass (*Nardus stricta*) which sheep do not like very much and which has little food value. Unfortunately for the sheep farmer, mat-grass covers very large areas of the uplands.

People who study the high sheepwalks have discovered that the pastures are changing for the worse as time goes on. This is because the sheep nibble so hard and often (do they ever stop eating?) at the fescues and bents that these grasses are weakened and get over-

12. Sheep have a big effect on the ecology of the uplands. Their close grazing prevents the growth of trees and many flowering plants.

whelmed by mat-grass of which the sheep eat so little. So it comes about that sheep, where they are too numerous, may spoil their own habitat by turning it into mat-grass moorland. This situation has got worse in recent years as Britain's eating habits have changed. Because people in general have more money than they used to have, they can afford to buy more lamb, which is young and tender but more expensive, and less of the older, tougher meat called mutton which is cheaper. So naturally farmers keep more lambs and fewer older sheep on the hills than they used to. And because lambs can eat only the tenderest grasses they take even less of the mat-grass than older sheep would. So this is a further reason why the mat-grass has been spreading.

During this century agricultural scientists have been studying the higher grasslands in the hope of changing them into better sheep pastures. By experiments in plant nurseries they have succeeded in breeding grasses which have greater food value than wild grasses have. So in recent years more and more hillsides have been ploughed and fertilised, then sown with the seeds of the better grasses. You can often pick out these improved pastures from a distance because they are much greener than the older pasture nearby, especially if the old pasture is of mat-grass, which is pale, almost whitish, much of the year. In the newly made pastures the mountain wild flowers are, of course, absent. This is depressing for naturalists. But to most farmers wild flowers in their pastures are only weeds. Still, there are a few who dislike the improved pastures because they believe that some of the 'weeds' are herbs of value for the health of livestock. The new grasses most commonly planted on the hills are selected types of perennial rye-grass (*Lolium perenne*).

So far we have looked only at the turf of well-drained slopes. But where drainage is poor and the ground almost permanently wet you may find a much larger, coarser species called purple moor-grass (*Molinia caerulea*). Instead of forming a turf that is easy to walk on, the moor-grass usually grows in big, knobbly tussocks and if you have to walk a mile or two over that sort of ground you can soon get tired as you stumble and flounder along. Wet land like this may be covered not by moor-grass but by another tall, tussocky species called tufted hair-grass (*Deschampsia cespitosa*); or by great tracts of soft rush (*Juncus effusus*). In some places you may find your boots sinking into real bog, but that is a habitat we will look at in Chapter 7.

What about the animals and birds of mountain grasslands? Let us begin with the more obvious insects you are likely to meet with as you walk over the hills. Large hairy caterpillars for instance, like those of the drinker moth (*Philudoria potatoria*), the northern eggar (*Lasiocampa quercus callunae*) and the fox moth (*Macrothylacia rubi*) are common and conspicuous, not hiding by day as so many caterpillars

60

do. The drinker is mainly dark-grey; the eggar is brown with black bands; the fox is tawny with black rings. Fox caterpillars are particularly abundant in some years and very noticeable because they lie sluggishly about the grass. Of these three species the drinker alone lives on grass; the other two eat the heather and bilberry that often grow amongst the grass. As for the moths, the eggar and the fox are diurnal: you may see the males dashing wildly about the grasslands or heather moors on sunny days. But the drinker is a night-flier and your best hope of seeing it is when it is attracted to a light.

In June or earlier you may occasionally find the high grasslands crawling with the glossy, dark-brown little caterpillars of the antler moth (*Cerapteryx graminis*) which in plague years have been known to eat whole hillsides bare of any grass. To find them you should keep an eye on birds of the crow family: in June the rooks (*Corvus frugilegus*), jackdaws (*Corvus monedula*) and carrion crows bring their young to the hills every day to feed on caterpillars of the antler moth and other insects. Click beetles (*Elateridae*), for example, are sometimes very abundant in the mountain turf. They are long, narrow and brown. Their larvae are yellowish wire worms, root-eaters unpopular with farmers and gardeners. Large black beetles crawling boldly about the turf are dor beetles (*Geotrupes stercorarius*), a common prey of kestrels. You will find the wing-cases of these and other beetles in the regurgitated pellets which kestrels leave below fence posts and other perches.

There are very few species of butterflies on the uplands but one that is very abundant up to about 600 m (1970 ft) is the small heath (*Coenonympha pamphilus*). You will find this little red-brown butterfly on the wing from May to September in various open habitats but mainly on the grasslands because grass is its food-plant. Another pretty little butterfly, the green hairstreak (*Callophrys rubi*), brown above and green on the underside, you may meet with here and there on the semi-uplands where its food plants, bilberry, gorse or broom (*Sarothamnus scoparius*), are not far away. In Scotland, likewise on not very high ground, you may see a dark-brown butterfly with a reddish band across the wings. This is the Scotch argus (*Erebia aethiops*) whose caterpillars live on grasses.

61

13. The green hairstreak butterfly (*Callophrys rubi*) is brown on the upperside of its wings and green below. It is local on hillsides and moorland edges.

Four very small mammals may be common in mountain grass-lands: field vole, wood mouse (*Apodemus sylvaticus*), common shrew (*Sorex araneus*) and pygmy shrew (*Sorex minutus*). Field voles I mentioned in Chapter 5 as sometimes being super-abundant in newly fenced forestry plantations. But they can have population explosions even on unfenced sheepwalks. You will easily know if there are many voles about, for then their holes are everywhere in the grass. And though voles are nocturnal you will occasionally see them scuttle from one hole to another in broad daylight, a risky thing to do in a world where sharp-eyed buzzards and kestrels are often patrolling the sky in search of prey.

The wood mouse is badly named, for it lives in many places besides woods. But its other common name, fieldmouse, is no better because it is not restricted to fields either. The fact is that this little rodent is found almost everywhere. It is certainly a part of the world of a mountain, for it has been found on the tops of the Cairngorms, along with field voles. As for our two smallest insectivores, the shrews, both the common and pygmy range very high into the uplands (the pygmy shrew has been seen at the top of Ben Nevis). But you are not likely to

Fig. 20. Common shrew (*Sorex araneus*)

see shrews unless you happen to find a dead one because, like voles and mice, they are nocturnal. Their relation, the water shrew (*Neomys fodiens*), has been seen at lakes in the semi-uplands.

One insectivore easily detected is the mole (*Talpa europaea*). You probably won't see one but if any are present you will see their hills. So if you find any mole hills on high ground look carefully at your map, decide what the altitude is and make a note of it, because there is plenty still to be found out about the height to which moles and other small mammals ascend. In mapping their ranges take care not to be misled by any dead ones you may find: they could have been carried up from lower ground by some predator such as a buzzard.

The upland sheep country is far from rich in birds. The number of species is small and, except at certain seasons, the populations of these species are scanty. Among the largest and most obvious are raven (*Corvus corax*), carrion crow, hooded crow (*Corvus corone cornix*) (Scotland and Ireland), rook, jackdaw, magpie, buzzard and kestrel. Between them, mainly from spring to autumn, they eat quantities of grassland insects, worms and small mammals. In Wales two rare birds, chough (*Pyrrhocorax pyrrhocorax*) and kite (*Milvus*

63

milvus), also live on these grasslands. The chough, though mainly coastal, inhabits some hill districts also, picking up ants, spiders and similar tiny prey. The kite snatches anything edible: worms, voles, moles, small birds and offal. On the sheepwalks of Scotland you might well see golden eagles (*Aquila chrysaetos*) circling over in search of mountain hares.

Carrion too is important in the diet of eagles. When a sheep dies on the hills it is not buried as dead animals are on lowland farms. Instead it becomes a feast for birds of prey, ravens and crows. So many sheep die every year that we can safely say that sheep farming plays a key part in the lives of these large mountain birds by keeping them generously supplied with mutton. In summer you will find plenty of skylarks and meadow pipits on grassy hills but they nearly all move down in autumn to pass the winter in the nearby lowlands; or they migrate far away. So you can walk over the uplands in winter and see hardly a small bird all day unless you are lucky enough to meet with a flock of snow buntings (*Plectrophenax nivalis*). They come to the British Isles in autumn from far northern breeding places.

It isn't until the last days of March that the mountain grasslands begin to liven up as the breeding snipe (*Gallinago gallinago*), curlews (*Numenius arquata*), lapwings (*Vanellus vanellus*), wheatears, sky-larks and meadow pipits arrive. Gradually they spread out over the hills, each male bird working hard to claim a territory by much singing and driving away of rivals. Though it breeds in various other habitats the curlew is perhaps commonest on damp, semi-upland grasslands, especially where there are stretches of soft rush or purple moor grass. In that zone of country, from March to July, the yodelling of the curlew is the best known bird voice of the grasslands. In the evening the drumming of the snipe is also a characteristic sound.

Easily commonest of all hill birds are the pipits and the larks. The male meadow pipit flutters steeply and silently high into the air, then glides straight back to earth in song. The skylark stays airborne, circling and singing. In fine weather in spring or early summer you can walk the grasslands all day and never be away from the music of larks and pipits. You will find both of them most abundant where the grass is tall enough to hide their nests. In some high grassy valleys you will also find cuckoos, for they lay their eggs in meadow pipits' nests and like to feed on grassland caterpillars, especially hairy ones such as the drinker.

While larks and pipits prefer the rougher grasslands, the wheatear has a decided preference for very short turf where it hops about quickly, picking up its insect food. So it is indebted to the sheep which keep the grass well grazed. And not only the grass. If you look closely you will often find nibbled heather among the grass. So if the sheep were taken away for two or three years that sort of ground would change into heather moor and the whole ecology of the place would be different. How different, we shall discover in the next chapter.

Fig. 21. Wheatear (*Oenanthe oenanthe*)

7. Peat Bogs and Heather Moors

In the last chapter we saw that the biggest stretches of mountain grassland consist largely of sheep's fescue, common bent and mat-grass; and that where the soil is wetter you might find yourself staggering over hummocks of purple moor-grass. But even worse can follow. You may come to ground that is too boggy for purple moor-grass but just right for another abundant plant, cottongrass, that is

14. Peat bogs are common in high-rainfall areas. They have special plants such as sundews (*Drosera* spp.) and are a breeding place for birds like dunlin (*Calidris alpina*) and golden plover (*Pluvialis apricaria*).

easily named in summer when its seeding heads are so fluffy with 'cotton' that whole areas are white with it. You will soon spot that there are two kinds of cottongrass in these upland bogs. They are easily distinguished because one, common cottongrass (*Eriophorum angustifolium*), has several cottony heads to a plant and the other, hare's-tail cottongrass (*Eriophorum vaginatum*), has only one. Note also that 'cottongrass', like so many old country names, is very misleading. The plant is in fact a sedge, not a grass.

Some boggy hollows are covered not by cottongrass but by bog moss (sphagnum, plural sphagna). There are many species of sphagna and they nearly all make green cushions on wet ground or grow in or under water. You should be careful where you walk in sphagnum bogs because patches of moss that look quite firm may in fact be floating on deep mire.

Among the interesting plants you are most likely to find in bogs are the sundews. Small and white-flowered, they catch and kill flies on their sticky foliage and then, sucking the flies' juices through the

15. Great sundew (*Drosera anglica*). Sundews catch insects on their sticky leaves, kill them with acid juices and then digest them, so obtaining nitrogen not available to their roots in the infertile peat bogs where they grow.

leaves, they digest them. By getting their food in this extraordinary way the sundews can exist in quite infertile acid soil. They can even grow without any soil at all, their roots being merely anchored among wet leaves of bog moss. There are three species. Most abundant is the round-leaved sundew (*Drosera rotundifolia*), usually less than 10 cm tall, and easily known by its circular leaves. Scarcest is the oblong-leaved sundew (*Drosera intermedia*), smaller than common sundew and distinguished by its narrow leaves. Largest is the great sundew (*Drosera anglica*), whose strongholds are the Scottish Highlands and north-west Ireland. In most other districts it is local or scarce. It looks like an outsize version of oblong-leaved sundew and may reach 25 cm (10 in) or more. But it is often much smaller than that.

A very beautiful bog plant is a lily called bog asphodel (*Narthecium ossifragum*), which has bright yellow flowers in July followed by colourful orange seed pods. Typical neighbours of asphodel are: a pink-flowered, bog-loving heather called cross-leaved heath (*Erica tetralix*); a frail-looking, straggling plant known as cranberry which has pink, bell-shaped flowers and edible, bright-red berries; and there are a few sedges, two of which, deergrass (*Scirpus cespitosus*) and white beak-sedge (*Rhynchospora alba*), can be so abundant and mat-like as to exclude most other plants. Shallow pools in acid bogs are often overgrown by a handsome plant called bogbean (*Menyanthes trifoliata*) whose leaves and pink-white flowers stand well above the water surface. Or the pool may be totally covered by a floating mat of leaves of bog pondweed (*Potamogeton polygonifolius*). What all these bog plants have in common is a dislike of lime (calcium carbonate) in the soil or water in which they grow. Most of highland Britain is covered by lime-deficient soils but this limelessness or acidity (what farmers often call sourness) is most pronounced in bogs. It is usually the centre of a bog that is most acid and infertile, whereas the margins receive a little fertility by drainage from the better soil surrounding the bog. The result is that on the edges of a bog you will often find plants which, though true bog species, cannot live in the extremely sour conditions of bog centres. Such plants are lousewort (*Pedicularis sylvatica*), lesser spearwort (*Ranunculus flammula*), marsh violet (*Viola palustris*), marsh St. John's wort

16. (*left*) Bog asphodel (*Narthecium ossifragum*), a member of the lily family, has bright yellow flowers and is common in some upland peat bogs.
17. (*right*) Butterwort (*Pinguicula vulgaris*) is, like the sundews, a plant which catches insects on its leaves. It is frequent in wet places in mountain country.

(*Hypericum elodes*), marsh cinquefoil (*Potentilla palustris*), marsh speedwell (*Veronica scutellata*), heath spotted-orchid (*Dactylorhiza maculata*), marsh pennywort (*Hydrocotyle vulgaris*), lesser skullcap (*Scutellaria minor*) and sneezewort (*Achillea ptarmica*).

You can find boglands in almost any sort of country where drainage is poor and there is no lime in the soil. But such bogs are especially common on moorland in high rainfall areas, the sort of place where heather is also most abundant. So bogs and heather moors often merge into one another, the heather growing best where the drainage is comparatively good, leaving the waterlogged hollows for the bog plants.

69

What bogs and heather moors usually have in common is peat, a very interesting type of soil which has been much studied by ecologists. When you dig it out of a bog it is spongy with water and practically black. But when dried it turns brown and then you can see more clearly what it is made of. It obviously isn't much like ordinary soil because it is full of strands or fibres of only slightly rotted plants. They do not decay because in a bog there are not enough oxygen and bacteria to produce decomposition.

So anything that gets buried deeply in peat is likely to be preserved almost intact for a very long time. Even soft plants like bog moss can be identified when brought up from the lowest levels of a peat bog where they have lain for thousands of years. The same with the pollen of prehistoric trees: it too can be named and so can tell us a great deal about the forests which used to cover most of our uplands except the very highest ground. And from bones found embedded in peat we learn about the cattle, the elk and other animals which were once wild in the British Isles.

Traces of human history have also been found in peat bogs— ancient ornaments, tools, weapons and the remains of domestic animals. Sometimes human bodies complete with clothing have been dug out of peat where they have been preserved for well over a thousand years. So, containing all this evidence of the past, a peat bog is a truly valuable out-door museum.

In Chapter 2 we looked at erosion and saw how even the very hardest rocks get worn away at last. You can imagine how easily this can happen to soft stuff like peat. So as you explore the uplands look out for eroded peat moors. Where weathering has been particularly severe you will find yourself walking along channels lined with cliffs of black, wet peat that are taller than yourself. In such places you see how deep the peat is and, very likely, if you search you will find remains of twigs, branches and trunks of prehistoric trees still with the bark intact and identifiable, probably as birch or pine.

Because it burns well when dried, peat has until this century been a universal fuel for the people of highland Britain to use on their fires. In summer it was cut into brick-shaped pieces, built into stacks to dry it and then taken home in autumn. This practice continues only here

18. The peat blanket which covers great areas of the uplands is being eroded away in many places.

and there in Great Britain, but in western Ireland you will see people cutting peat (they call it turf) as they have always done. In Ireland they have such vast deposits of peat that it is used for producing electricity in power stations. Another big modern use for peat is for horticulture.

Peat can be excavated in large quantities only where its beds are deep (they go down 10 metres (33 ft) in some places). But outside these deep bogs there are layers of peat called blanket bog lying up and down the slopes of vast areas of the uplands and they form the typical country of the heather moors. Finally we should note that in the north of England and in Scotland peat bogs are often called mosses.

Before we venture into the wide, breezy spaces of the heather moors we had better decide exactly what plant we mean by heather. We have already met one kind of heather, the cross-leaved heath which grows in the bogs. But there are two other heathers which are

71

much more conspicuous. First there is common heather (*Calluna vulgaris*). This is the pale purple heather of the vast peaty uplands of highland Britain, the heather that colours the grouse moors in August and September. It is widespread from near sea level up to about 1,000 m. Above that, on those high mountains where the vegetation is clearly zoned, as on the Cairngorms, heather gives place to the bilberry–crowberry zone. Another heather species is bell heather (*Erica cinerea*). It is also abundant, especially on rocks, but does not make great spreads across the peat moors as common heather does; and it reaches to only about 670 m (2200 ft). The flowers of bell heather open a good month earlier than those of common heather and are easily distinguished by their rich red-purple.

Upland heather moors are a home for some noteworthy moths (many of which are also found on lowland heathlands). Perhaps the best known is the emperor (*Saturnia pavonia*), a large, spectacular

19. The emperor (*Saturnia pavonia*) is a large reddish-grey moth frequent on heather moors. Here a female has just emerged from her cocoon.

moth with colourful eye-spots both on its fore and hind wings. The male emperors can be seen by day flying fast over the moorland in early spring, seeking the females which cling to heather stems and attract the males to them by powerful scent glands. In summer you may find the fully fed emperor caterpillars: they are large and bright green and banded with black and yellow. They pupate among the heather in a tough brown cocoon made of coarse silk. For the emperor belongs to the silk-moths, a mainly tropical family.

Here are the names of a few other heather moor moths: beautiful yellow underwing (*Anarta myrtilli*); true lover's knot (*Lycophotia varia*) which has a complicated pattern of white lines on its purple forewings; clouded buff (*Diacrisia sannio*); wood tiger (*Parasemia plantaginis*); ruby tiger (*Phragmatobia fuliginosa*); July highflier (*Hydriomena furcata*); and usually most abundant of all, the common heath (*Ematurga atomaria*), which from May to August you may disturb from heather wherever you walk.

You will find very few species of butterfly on upland heather moors. As on grasslands the small heath is the most likely wherever you go because it is at home in so many habitats and may well be Britain's commonest butterfly. Its cousin, the much more local large heath (*Coenonympha tullia*), also ranges up to about 600 m (1950 ft). It is found from mid-Wales and Shropshire northwards and lives where heather is well mixed with other bog plants including grasses. In August the flowering heather is visited by numbers of small tortoiseshells and in some years red admirals (*Vanessa atalanta*) which fly up from the lowlands for the nectar feast as many other insects do. And anywhere on the hills in summer you may see the large white butterfly (*Pieris brassicae*), a great traveller which is undeflected from its course by mountain ranges.

A striking insect of heather moors (except in Ireland) is the golden-ringed dragonfly (*Cordulegaster boltoni*), one of our largest and most powerful species. Boldly banded yellow and black, it is usually seen flying swiftly in pursuit of flies; but in wet weather it may be found clinging limply to heather stems. On warm days you won't fail to notice the many wild bees noisy among the heather flowers. You may see honey bees (*Apis mellifera*) too, because the flow of nectar is so

73

20. On Dartmoor, Devon, rounded granite hillocks called tors are a feature of the landscape.

copious that some beekeepers take their hives to the moors in August, for heather honey has a specially delicious flavour.

About flies I will say nothing except that if you go camping don't forget your midge repellant. In the Scottish Highlands midges (*Ceratopogonidae*) and other biting flies are such a scourge that the deer keep to the highest ground in summer to escape them. But even midges are useful. They are a food for dragonflies (*Odonata*); and midge larvae are part of the diet of many aquatic animals.

A bird that belongs more than any other to the upland heather is the red grouse (*Lagopus lagopus*). Its chief food is shoots of heather and to help in the digestion of this tough food the grouse also eats sharp grit which assists the grinding up of food in its gizzard. Nearly a quarter of the grouse's food is animal, mostly insects, including the heather beetle (*Lochmaea suturalis*) which, if very numerous, does widespread damage to moorland heather. The red-brown grouse are well hidden when feeding among the dark twigs of the heather. If you disturb them they rise with whirring wings and usually call out a loud, rapid *gobàk-gobàk-gobàk* as they fly fast and low across the moorland, a lovely wild cry to hear breaking the silence of the hills. This grouse is one of the hardiest of birds, enduring the long rains and snows of winter in very exposed places as high as 900 m.

Fig. 22. Red grouse (*Lagopus lagopus*)

Grouse are classed along with pheasants (*Phasianus colchicus*) and partridges (*Perdix perdix*) as game birds. This means that for a part of the year they are not protected by law and can be shot for sport. Because sportsmen are willing to pay a lot of money to be allowed to kill these birds, grouse-shooting (it lasts from August 12 to December 10) has become big business. So the best grouse-moors, most of which are in the north of England and Scotland, are kept as private as possible and the grouse are carefully watched over by gamekeepers.

75

Other birds typical of the heather moors are meadow pipit (very common); twite (*Acanthis flavirostris*), which is locally numerous in Scotland and northern England and has recently spread south into the Midlands and Wales; a small, very speedy falcon, the merlin (*Falco columbarius*), which preys on pipits, daylight-flying moths and other small creatures; the golden plover (*Pluvialis apricaria*), whose piping notes are among the most delightful sounds of the moorlands in spring; and the dunlin (*Calidris alpina*), a small wader which usually conceals its eggs in grass or heather near upland lakes. On some moors, especially in Scotland, you should look out for a large and graceful raptor called the hen harrier (*Circus cyaneus*) which may be pale grey (the male) or dark-brown (the female).

Also on Scottish heather moors you may be lucky enough to see a golden eagle: for when not hunting for mountain hares or eating dead sheep, the Scottish eagles are likely to be looking for grouse. Eggs of the grouse, though well camouflaged to be hidden among the heather, are sometimes discovered and sucked by crows.

The mountain, or blue, hare (*Lepus timidus*) on which eagles often prey, though ranging widely over the uplands, is most abundant on heather moors, for heather is its favourite food. Commonest in eastern Scotland it is the one mammal of Great Britain that is found only on mountains, apart from the few domesticated reindeer (*Rangifer tarandus*) of the Cairngorms (brought there in 1952). On lower ground the mountain hare presumably cannot compete for food with the larger common, or brown, hare (*Lepus europaeus*). In Ireland things are different: because the brown hare is virtually absent there, the mountain hare occupies lowland as well as upland habitats. A noteworthy feature of the mountain hare is that in Scotland it usually turns white in winter, as the ptarmigan (*Lagopus mutus*) does. Turning white is a trick used by cold-climate animals and birds all round the world to help them to hide in the snow. In Ireland, where there is much less snow than in the Scottish Highlands, the mountain hares seldom turn white.

Britain's largest wild mammal, the red deer, includes heather in its varied diet; and heather moors are an important part of the Scottish deer forests. But more about them in Chapter 9. The only other sizeable mammal of the heather is an astonishing one: for many years since they escaped from captivity on a nearby estate a colony of red-necked wallabies (*Wallabia rufogrisea*) (their native land is Australia) has been living wild and free on a heather moor in the Peak District National Park between Leek and Buxton.

If you are on the hills in late winter or early spring you will sometimes see stretches of the moorland on fire. These fires are not accidental or the result of vandalism but are deliberate. Gamekeepers burn the heather to prevent it from growing up into tall straggly bushes whose young shoots would not be easily reached by grouse. Where the heather is burnt the new shoots spring from the roots at ground level where the grouse can graze on them without difficulty. The moors are burnt methodically one section each year, so that there is always plenty of old heather to serve as cover for the birds.

Sheep farmers also burn heather but their aim is to get rid of it in the hope that grass will take its place. They also burn grasslands in the belief that if the old dead grass is burnt off in winter the young grass will be more quickly accessible to the sheep in spring. But in the long run moor burning may be very wasteful because many of the ashes of the burnt plants are either blown away by the wind or carried away into the streams—a loss of valuable chemicals from a habitat which can ill afford it.

8. Springs, Streams and Lakes

Our mountains, especially those on the western side of Britain and Ireland, are prodigious rain-makers. This is because most winds come across the Atlantic ocean and are heavily laden with moisture. When all this wet air is cooled, as it is when rising over the uplands, it often condenses into clouds and rain. So even when the lowlands are sunny, the inland hills can be hidden behind curtains of wet weather. This sort of upland rain is called orographic rain (from the Greek word *oros* which means mountain).

A few figures will help us to see what great differences there are between the rainfall of lowland and highland Britain. The average rainfall in the driest regions of Britain (which are on the east coast) is less than 500 mm (20 in) a year. But the average rainfall on some of our wettest mountains is about 5,000 mm (200 in) a year. Sometimes extraordinary figures have been recorded: 6,248 mm (250 in) on Snowdon in 1912, for example.

After rain the lowlands soon dry out in the warmth of the summer sun which draws the moisture back up into the air. But on mountains there is much less evaporation because up there the air is cooler and the sun often hidden behind clouds. Here then is another reason, besides the high rainfall, why boggy ground is so common on the hills and why streams and lakes are everywhere.

Have you ever tried to trace a river back to its source? If so you have probably found it a real puzzle, because what you usually find when you get near the head of the river is that it divides into several branches and it is then hard to decide which one to call the main stream.

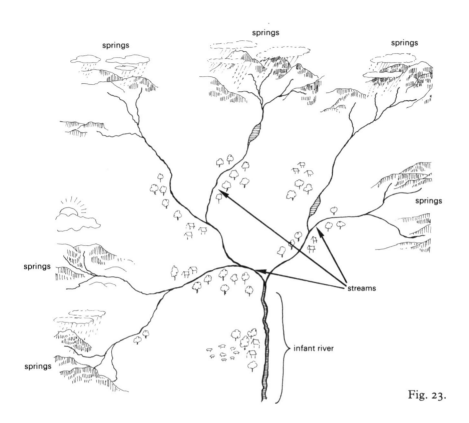

springs

springs

springs

springs

springs

springs

streams

infant river

Fig. 23.

Another thing you will find out about the various sources of your river is that they don't start at the top of the mountain. Instead they first appear as springs flowing out of the slopes. This is because a lot of the rain that falls on the mountain sinks into cracks and seeps down deep into the rocks. The fact is that mountains are not as solid as they look. They have been so shaken up by the earth pressures of all past ages that they are full of crannies down which water can find its way. And many rocks are not only cracked but porous. Though they look hard and dry they contain tiny cavities (pores) in which water collects. So the rocks inside a mountain may be permanently soaked

79

with water, which explains why even after weeks of drought the streams continue to flow. These reservoirs of water stored away in the rocks are known as groundwater, as distinct from the water of streams, rivers and lakes which is surface water.

Inside the mountain the groundwater works its way by force of gravity through the porous rocks until it reaches a non-porous (or impermeable) layer. It can now go no further vertically. Instead it is forced to flow out of the sides of the mountain in the form of springs.

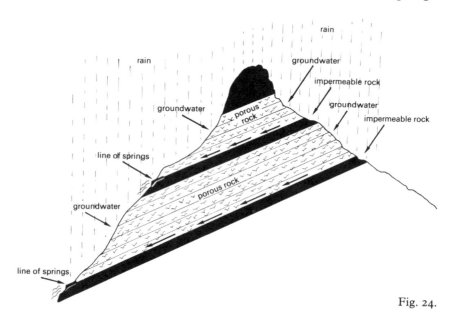

Fig. 24.

In some places the water that springs out of a mountainside spreads out to form a patch of waterlogged ground. Botanists call such marshy spots 'flushes' and these are often a habitat for rather special plants which enjoy gently seeping water that has plenty of oxygen in it and also minerals dissolved out of the rock inside the mountain. But often a spring, instead of forming a flush, comes out of the hillside as a strong gush that immediately forms a streamlet which in maybe only a few hundred metres joins other streamlets to form a stream (called a burn in Scotland and the north of England). These high-level streams are usually fast flowing (except where they wind sluggishly across flattish peat moors) and soon unite with others to form the upper reaches of infant rivers.

Apart from being much smaller, mountain streams are different in many ways from lowland rivers. For instance, their levels rise and fall very quickly. In heavy rain they can change in a couple of hours from the merest trickles into dangerous torrents. Then very soon after the rain has stopped the flood begins to go down and by next day the stream has died away to a trickle as before. These short quick floods are called spates; and streams on which they are especially common are called spate streams.

When you first look into a spate stream and see how rocky its bed is and how little vegetation there is in it you might well suppose that no fish or other animals could possibly live in all that rushing water. It is certainly true that, compared with a rich lowland stream, the animal populations of most high mountain streams are small. All the same you may be surprised how many little creatures do manage to get a living in a world of rock and spate water. Maybe life for them is not as dangerous as it looks. By keeping to the sheltered side of boulders or by hiding under stones or in aquatic mosses they mostly succeed in keeping out of harm's way. And if by chance they do get swept downstream they have a good chance of finding sheltered nooks where they can resume their way of life. Freshwater shrimps (*Gammarus* spp.), flatworms (*Turbellaria*), mites (*Acari*), mayflies (*Ephemeroptera*), stoneflies (*Plectoptera*), water beetles (*Coleoptera*), caddis flies (*Trichoptera*), gnats (*Culicidae*) and various other flies— these may be found, at some or all stages of their lives, in mountain torrents.

As for the fish of such lively waters, they too are small and are hiders under stones. You are not likely to find more than three kinds high in the uplands—brown trout (*Salmo trutta*), bullhead (*Cottus gobio*) and stone loach (*Noemacheilus barbatulus*)—and in the vast majority of streams there will be trout alone, often not more than the length of a human finger. For in waters where food is scarce the trout remain small all their lives. Yet if they were to be transferred to richer waters they would soon put on weight. A curious fact about some fish, as distinct from most other animals, is that provided they find enough food they go on getting bigger all their lives.

Though the world of a torrent may appear difficult to live in because of its coldness, the roughness of its water and a scarcity of food, yet it also offers advantages. Water so high in the uplands is likely to be pure because the operations of man, the great polluter, are mostly down in the lowlands, the region of towns, factories, mines and agriculture. Then there is oxygen, which all life needs. This the mountain streams have in abundance because so much air gets into them as they ripple over pebble beds, splash among boulders and leap down waterfalls.

As everywhere in nature the creatures of the mountain streams can be divided into the eaters and the eaten. Or to put this in a better way: animal Y eats animal Z; but X preys on Y; W lives on X; and so on. This is what we call a food chain. Near to the top of the chain in our stream we find the trout, for its eats almost anything smaller than itself. Above the trout in the food chain are the heron (*Ardea cinerea*) and the otter (*Lutra lutra*), both of which, although mainly lowlanders, frequently hunt up the mountain streams and certainly include trout in their diet.

Also foraging along the hill streams is a small bird called the dipper (*Cinclus cinclus*), which is a predator of the trout in the sense that it eats trout eggs if it can find where they are buried among shingle in the bed of the stream. The dipper is a bird to be marvelled at. If you found a dead one and you didn't know what it was I don't think you'd guess it was a water bird. You would be more likely to think it was some relation of the blackbird, because it is about that size and is mainly blackish with a white breast. There is just nothing about the appearance of a dipper, certainly no webbing on the feet, to suggest it spends much of its time under water seeking small creatures that live on the beds of fast streams.

You will find three other small birds along the hill streams in spring and summer. There is a lively wader called the common sandpiper (*Tringa hypoleucos*) which is brown above, white below and has an ever-bobbing stern. It does not dive into the stream like the dipper but eats small creatures picked out of the shallows. It hides its four delicately coloured eggs in river bank vegetation. The other two streamside birds are wagtails: the pied (*Motacilla alba*), which is also common in the lowlands; and the grey wagtail (*Motacilla cinerea*), which is commoner in the uplands and is distinguished by having a grey back, a yellow rump and yellow underparts. Like the sandpiper the wagtails are pickers up of tiny animals at the water's edge. In addition they often flutter up to take flying insects.

Many a mountain stream plunges sooner or later into a gorge. With high walls of rock keeping the sun out and with air that is damp with the spray of waterfalls, a gorge is just the place for ferns, mosses and liverworts. So it is in highland Britain that the largest numbers of these non-flowering plants are to be found.

On gorge sides more open to the light you will often find trees growing out of cracks in the rock, usually crooked trees leaning dangerously over the void. They can exist there but not on nearby hillsides because they are out of reach of the ever nibbling sheep. Their branches are often green with mosses and leafy lichens or they bristle with polypody ferns—all plants which love a perpetually damp atmosphere.

For a few months in autumn and winter some mountain streams become a home for two large kinds of fish: salmon (*Salmo salar*) and sea trout (or sewin) which is a migratory race of the brown trout. Just as some birds move each year from non-breeding areas to breeding areas so do some fish. Salmon and sea trout live much of their lives far away in the ocean. But they are all born in fresh water and so at breeding time the adults leave the ocean and swim far up the rivers, some of them going right up into the hill country where the streams are so shallow that the back fins of the fish may stick up out of the water. They go up the streams because their eggs and young need water rich in oxygen in order to survive. We give salmon different names for the different stages of their growth. Newly hatched they are alevins. Then for a year they are fry. After that they become parr and in this stage have dark bars along their flanks. In hill streams it takes two or three years of feeding before they pass out of the parr stage and become the completely silver fish we call smolts. They have now reached a point in their development when they can go down to the sea, where the food is much richer than in the streams. Then, sometimes after only one year but normally after several, they return as adult salmon to the rivers where they were born. They are marvellous orienteers, finding their way back across hundreds of miles of ocean to exactly the right rivers. And as they swim upstream they even leap up waterfalls in their determination to get to their spawning grounds.

A high dam built across a river would prevent salmon and migrating trout from ever getting upstream to their spawning places. So to help them a fish pass is provided—a passage-way with water flowing down steps up which the fish find their way from one step to another. You can visit a famous Scottish fish pass at the hydro-electricity dam at Pitlochry in the Grampian Mountains near Perth. If you make inquiries you will find fish passes on other rivers too; and also traps which are used to catch fish in order to mark them for migration studies. By such experiments salmon tagged with identity labels in our rivers have been caught again far out to sea— providing a valuable clue to their movements and life history.

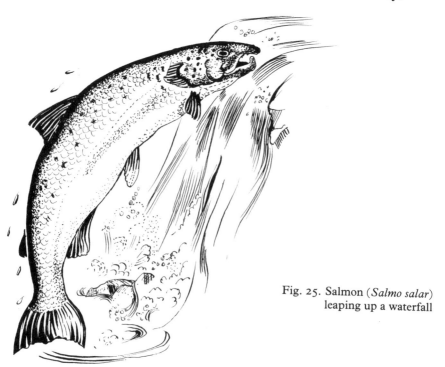

Fig. 25. Salmon (*Salmo salar*) leaping up a waterfall

A glance at a map of highland Britain will show you that the streams flow into and out of hundreds of lakes (called lochs in Scotland, loughs in Ireland, both words being pronounced like the English word 'lock' but ending huskily). In Welsh a lake is a llyn. In the Lake District an upland lake is usually called a tarn. Lakes may be large but most are small. They can be very deep, of medium depth or very shallow. A few are nearly circular, many are long and narrow. Some are sheltered, others are exposed to the wind. Some are high and cold, others are lower and warmer. As you might expect, since lakes are all sizes, shapes and depths and lie at various altitudes, no two are alike. Even a pair of lakes side by side and connected by a stream (a possible highway for animals and plants) may be found to have little in common. For instance, if one of them has a stony bed and clear water and its neighbour has a peaty bottom and red-brown water there will certainly be big differences in their natural history.

Let us look at two types of shallow upland lakes. First, one that in high summer is completely covered by vegetation. Round its soft, peaty margin are mats of quaking bog moss mixed with clumps of cottongrass, bogbean, soft rush and other bog species. This water-logged zone merges just off-shore with a belt of bottle sedge (*Carex rostrata*), water horsetail (*Equisetum fluviatile*), floating sweet-grass (*Glyceria fluitans*) and branched bur-reed (*Sparganium erectum*). The centre of the lake is occupied by yellow-flowered water lilies (*Nuphar lutea*) whose big leaves, along with the smaller leaves of pondweeds (*Potamogeton* spp.), cover the entire surface of the water. There are two observations we can make immediately about such a weedy lake: it must be shallow because deep lakes are never covered all over with plants; its floor is probably soft with mud or peat, otherwise these large plants would never have got rooted; and it must be fairly sheltered because in exposed lakes most plants are prevented by wave action from getting a root-hold. Note, by the way, that the reed beds so characteristic of the edges of lowland lakes are usually absent from mountain lakes.

One thing we can assume about a lake so choked with vegetation: it is well on the way to extinction. All these plants rotting down winter after winter will gradually fill it with mire until there is no clear water left and it becomes less and less suitable for the lilies, the sedges and the horsetails. Bog mosses will invade it from the edges and eventually cover it completely, turning it into a bright green quaking carpet of sphagna. And that is the end of our lake. If the bog is below the tree line the wind may bring seeds of willow (*Salix* spp.) and birch and gradually what was a lake and then a bog will turn into a wood.

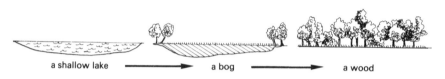

a shallow lake ⟶ a bog ⟶ a wood

Fig. 26. A natural succession

A series of changes of this sort by which one habitat turns into another and then into yet another is called a natural succession. Successions are always going on, many of them close to our own doorstep. But some of them are slow and we can easily miss them if we don't observe carefully.

The second type of shallow lake is one that we find in stony ground. In such a hard-floored lake, instead of tall plants sticking out of the water, what you are more likely to find is that the bed is thinly scattered with little green rosettes of narrow fleshy leaves. These plants can be quite confusing because five different species have adopted this form of life. They are shoreweed (*Littorella uniflora*), water lobelia (*Lobelia dortmanna*), awlwort (*Subularia aquatica*), common quillwort (*Isoetes lacustris*) and spring quillwort (*Isoetes echinospora*). Of these the easiest to name is the lobelia when in early summer it bears little violet flowers on slender stems that reach a few inches above the water. Shoreweed and the much rarer awlwort have inconspicuous flowers under the water; and the two quillworts, spore-bearing allies of the ferns and horsetails, do not flower at all. Because they have little vegetation to rot down in them, stony lakes change and disappear more slowly than peaty lakes. But if, as many do, they lie at the foot of a scree they can be gradually filled in by silt and pebbles from the streams that flow into them.

Besides shallow lakes there are deep lakes, including reservoirs made by man for water supplies, hydro-electricity or river flood control. These deeper waters are often poor in plant and animal life. Especially at high altitudes they are cold, windswept and usually acid; and below about four metres depth they are too dark for green plants to grow. A point to note about reservoirs is that to increase their water supplies they may be linked with lakes or streams in neighbouring valleys by aqueducts or tunnels. In this way animals and plants can make their way from one river system to another. Several kinds of fish, for instance, are known to have colonised new waters, unintentionally helped by engineering projects. Throughout nature there are opportunist species always ready to profit from situations which enable them to conquer new territory. Adaptability is the key to their success.

Nearly all upland lakes have fish in them but, as in the streams, the number of species is usually very small. In fact in some waters there is only one—the brown trout. Quite a lot of lakes also have three-spined sticklebacks (*Gasterosteus aculeatus*) and minnows (*Phoxinus phoxinus*). But in some lakes the minnows may be an introduction because anglers use them as live bait and sometimes tip in the unused ones at the end of the day's fishing. In a few deep lakes is a trout relative, the char (*Salvelinus alpinus*), the males of which develop red undersides in November and December, their breeding season. Pike (*Esox lucius*), perch (*Perca fluviatilis*) and eels (*Anguilla anguilla*) are found in some high-level waters but usually you have to come down into the valleys to find any other fish species. One interesting genus (group) of lake fishes belonging to the salmon family is known to science as *Coregonus*. In the British Isles, though not found in high mountain lakes, they are restricted to the highland region, but even there they are very local and have been given different popular names in their various districts. They are called pollan in Ireland (Lough Neagh and Lough Erne for instance). In Scotland they are powan (Loch Lomond and Loch Esk) or vendace (Lochmaben). In the Lake District they are known as schelly in Haweswater and Ullswater, and as vendace in Derwentwater. In Wales (Llyn Tegid, Bala) their name is gwyniad, which means 'shining white', a reference to the silvery colouring of all these fishes of the genus *Coregonus*.

21. Several closely related whitefish of the genus *Coregonus* are found in a few of the lakes of highland Britain. This is the gwyniad (*Coregonus lavaretus*) of Llyn Tegid, Bala, Wales.

The rate at which upland lake fish can grow depends on the abundance of the small aquatic animals on which they mostly feed. The more nutritious minerals there are dissolved in the water the greater the wealth of animal life. Search carefully in the shallows and your finds will probably include flatworms; water snails (*Mollusca*); leeches (*Hirudinea*) (don't worry, they are unlikely to be the medicinal sort that attacks man); various crustaceans; insects or the larvae of insects such as water beetles, water boatmen (*Notonecta* spp.), stoneflies, mayflies, dragonflies, gnats and midges; frog (*Rana temporaria*) and toad (*Bufo bufo*) tadpoles; newts (in the uplands usually the palmate newt (*Triturus helveticus*)); and very small fish and fish eggs. Because most upland lakes have acid water they are usually not rich in animal species. But if you examine a lake in limestone country you will find a greater variety, especially of molluscs (such as snails) and crustaceans (such as shrimps) for they need plenty of lime (calcium) to form their shells and skeletons. So the freshwater shrimp is commonest in calcium-rich waters and usually absent from very acid lakes and streams.

What birds you will discover on mountain lakes will depend first of all on altitude. Don't expect many on high-level lakes because they contain too little food. In most districts you need to come down to the lower moorlands to find lakes with populations of breeding birds. On some northern Scottish lochs are two very attractive birds, the red-throated (*Gavia stellata*) and black-throated (*Gavia arctica*) divers, and, more widespread, a typical northern duck, the wigeon (*Anas penelope*). A few moorland lochs have goosanders (*Mergus merganser*) but most of these saw-billed ducks breed on lower waters with trees nearby. Also on some lochs you will see colonies of common gulls (*Larus canus*). In the far north of Scotland you might be lucky enough to see truly wild grey lag geese (*Anser anser*) which breed by some lochs. All over the British moorlands the commonest breeding waterfowl are mallard (*Anas platyrhynchos*) and teal (*Anas crecca*); and the most characteristic lakeside wader is the common sandpiper. Some quite high lakes are regularly visited by cormorants (*Phalacrocorax carbo*) and herons; but the famous ospreys (*Pandion haliaetus*), increasing numbers of which now breed in Scotland, are tree-nesters and so are restricted to waters in the lowlands or the semi-uplands.

Widespread but thinly scattered on moorland lakes throughout the British Isles are colonies of black-headed gulls (*Larus ridibundus*). Most of them breed on islands but some place their nests in weedy shallows. If you discover such a colony or if you find the nests of any other birds you should go away immediately and let the parents come back, because eggs and young quickly get chilled in the cold air of the uplands.

9. Life is Hard at the Top

Ours is a thickly populated country where habitats untouched by man are rare. So we should put a high value on the summits, cliffs and screes of the mountains because some of them come very near to being quite natural, especially the cliffs. Centuries of grazing by sheep have altered the grasslands and heather moors. But mercifully sheep cannot climb vertical crags and though at times they venture along dangerous ledges they don't usually get very far and most plants are safe from their nibblings. Goats are more agile, so it is lucky that there are not many of them left on Britain's uplands. Any goats you see on our mountains are not genuine wild goats but goats gone wild—they are the descendants of domesticated herds once kept commonly on the mountains.

Here and there human rock climbers have no doubt done a little harm through an activity they call 'gardening', by which is meant clearing vegetation off the climbs in order to get a better footing on the rock. Fortunately climbers prefer the very hardest rocks where plants are fewest, so the damage on most climbs isn't serious. Much more harm has been done to our mountain flora by plant collectors, especially in the past. People are more conservation-minded these days, but in the last century there was a craze for collecting natural history specimens of all sorts. Mountain plants were gathered in quantity on the more accessible uplands by botanists and gardeners. Three rare ferns, for instance, holly fern (*Polystichum lonchitis*) and two small species called alpine woodsia (*Woodsia alpina*) and oblong woodsia (*Woodsia ilvensis*), were especially sought after and soon became even rarer as a result.

For botanists the most productive type of crag consists of half-rotten rock rich in minerals, especially lime or, in some places, potash or magnesia, a crag that has crumbled into countless ledges, holes and fissures where fertile soil has gathered from the weathering of the rock. In such a soil, provided there is perennial water seeping through it to counteract the drying effects of the mountain winds, plants of many kinds can root deeply and spread luxuriantly.

When you've visited a site like that you will be able to contrast it with those crags whose rocks are lime-less, especially the very hard rocks such as grits, granites, rhyolites and slates. They are often quite bare of vegetation or have a mere crusting of lichens; or, if they are well covered with vegetation, it is only a monotonous blanket of heather, bilberry, crowberry and similar dwarf shrubs.

Unfortunately these lime-less rocks, many of them extremely ancient, cover most of the British uplands. It is only here and there that you will find crags and screes (rarely whole mountains) whose soils are fertile enough to support a really varied community of mountain plants. Terms often used by ecologists to describe these better rocks include 'alkaline', 'lime-rich', 'calcareous' (from calcium), 'basic' and 'base-rich'. (Base is a word used in chemistry: calcium, magnesium and potassium are typical bases.) The other group of rocks, poor in plant species, are variously known as 'lime-deficient', 'limeless', 'base-poor', 'acid' and 'siliceous'. (Siliceous means rich in silica, one of the commonest elements of the earth's crust. Sandstones, grits, mudstones, slates and many other lime-deficient rocks are siliceous.)

We have special words to describe the plants that grow in these two types of habitat. A species that prefers a lime-rich soil is a calcicole (which means 'lime-inhabiting'). In contrast a plant which cannot flourish in lime-rich soil is a calcifuge (which means 'lime-avoiding'). Some plants are neither calcicoles nor calcifuges: they seem quite able to flourish whether the soil is base-rich or base-poor.

The cliff vegetation is usually best developed on crags that look north or east, because it needs perennial water and in that position it escapes the droughting effects of sun from the south and of prevailing winds from the south-west. It is true that by facing north or east the plants have to stand up to the coldest types of weather: but in the choice between two evils, cold or drought, it is drought that is worst. The plants of mountains have learnt to live with cold weather. They are plants which grow also in the tundra of the Arctic and many also grow high in the Alps. For this reason these tough species are called arctic-alpines.

Let us now look at a few typical arctic-alpine plants. First, the purple saxifrage (*Saxifraga oppositifolia*), which is locally abundant on high-level, lime-rich rocks in Scotland, the Lake District, Yorkshire, Wales and Ireland. One of the most beautiful of our mountain flowers, this saxifrage blooms weeks, sometimes months, earlier than most of its fellow alpines, its cushions of bright purple blooms often being fully out by Easter and occasionally as early as mid-February. Lime-loving arctic-alpines like the purple saxifrage are seldom found on their own. If conditions are right for one species they are suitable for others as well. So on the same ledge as you spot your purple saxifrage you may find several other typical arctic-alpines such as roseroot (*Sedum rosea*), mountain sorrel (*Oxyria digyna*), moss campion (*Silene acaulis*), mossy saxifrage (*Saxifraga hypnoides*), mountain avens (*Dryas octopetala*), alpine saw-wort (*Saussurea alpina*), alpine meadow-rue (*Thalictrum alpinum*), alpine cinquefoil (*Potentilla crantzii*) and green spleenwort (*Asplenium viride*). In other words you have discovered an arctic-alpine plant community, just as in the lowlands you might find a woodland community, a sea-shore community or a railway-bank community— groups of species which are often in each other's company because they share a liking for the same conditions.

There are many other plants of mountain base-rich rocks that you will get to know about as you widen your experience. As for the plants of base-poor rocks, some I have mentioned already—the great spreaders such as heather, bell heather, bilberry and crowberry. To these could be added mat-formers such as cloudberry (*Rubus chamaemorus*) and bearberry and, more local, alpine bearberry (*Arctous alpinus*) and bog bilberry (*Vaccinium uliginosum*). There is also parsley fern (*Cryptogramma crispa*) which makes a bright green carpet across many an acid scree.

22 and 23. Purple saxifrage
(*Saxifraga oppositifolia*) is a
beautiful arctic-alpine of lime-rich
mountain rocks. It flowers in late
winter and early spring, often amid
snow and icicles.

24. Cowberry (*Vaccinium vitis-idaea*) is frequent on moorlands. Its flowers are little white hanging bells and its berries are red and acid.

Many of the low-growing, mat-forming shrubs of mountains belong to the family Ericaceae and are often called ericaceous plants. They include heather, bilberry, cranberry, cowberry (*Vaccinium vitis-idaea*), bearberry, bog rosemary (*Andromeda polifolia*) and trailing azalea (*Loiseleuria procumbens*), and most have flowers like little hanging bells. We have seen how important heather is for wildlife, but some of the others are too, especially bilberry. Its flowers appear in March and April and are visited by the year's first flying insects. In summer its many fruits are eaten not only by typical upland birds like grouse and ring ouzel (*Turdus torquatus*) but also by woodpigeons, mistle thrushes and others which come up from the valleys for this annual feast. Mammals (even carnivores) eat them and you'll find fox droppings in summer purple with bilberry juice. Bilberry fruits best where sheep can't get at it: in the early stages of a

94

forestry plantation for instance, before the trees overshade it.

Perhaps you may wonder why it is that some plants live only on mountains? To answer this question we must again go back to the Ice Age. Because the ice-sheets did not extend south of the Thames we can suppose that what are now England's southernmost counties were then covered by a tundra vegetation similar to that found today at the southern edge of the Arctic: plants such as purple saxifrage, moss campion, mountain avens, dwarf willow (*Salix herbacea*) and other very hardy species. Then as the ice-sheet retreated these arctic-type plants followed it northwards across England until eventually they invaded Wales, the Lake District, Scotland and Ireland (for Ireland was still connected with Britain by dry land just as England was connected with the Continent).

Meanwhile conditions continued to get milder and this encouraged a whole range of less hardy plants to advance into south England from the Continent. So as the climate became less suitable for arctic-alpine plants, they gradually got elbowed out of nearly all lowland regions. Eventually they found that almost the only places where they could hold off the invaders were the higher mountains, because up there they had the advantage of being better able to stand the harsher climate. And there we still find them today.

But it is only the very highest and bleakest places that these arctic-alpines have to themselves. For although the mountain weather can be very cold at times, the British climate as a whole is mild compared with that of the Arctic or the Alps, and it is only about half a dozen times in a century that we get a really severe winter. The result is that many lowland plants have managed to invade the uplands, some to over 900 m (2950 ft). Many of them are better known as wild flowers of lowland woodlands, especially woods with base-rich soils. Under the trees they flourish in cool shade with their roots in rich humus: and these are much like the conditions they find in summer on the moist, cool ledges of sunless, north-facing, lime-rich mountain crags. So don't be surprised, when you've scrambled up to the cliffs of some high corrie, to discover that your arctic-alpines are mixed up with primroses, wood anemones, red campion (*Silene dioica*), herb-Robert (*Geranium robertianum*), wood-sorrel, dog's mercury (*Mercurialis*

95

perennis), moschatel (*Adoxa moschatellina*), early purple orchid (*Orchis mascula*) and a host of other lowlanders. Remember that the now treeless uplands were once covered to a great height with woodlands or scrub until climatic change and the hand of man turned them into pastures. Many a high crag now remote from tree-cover once rose straight out of forests of oak, birch, willow and pine. Keep that picture in mind and you won't find it strange to see so many woodland plants on the ledges. Just as the arctic-alpine species are a relic of the tundra that once covered all Britain, so the woodland plants are a memory of the broad-leaved forests that came in as the tundra retreated.

How, you may ask, do mountain plants manage to live through the terrible conditions of some really hard winter when even our normally mild coastal regions suffer weeks of penetrating frost? In the Arctic, the Alps and other very high places, a large part of the answer is that the plants survive because they are sheltered from the intense cold by a blanket of snow which gets thicker and thicker as winter goes on. Perhaps you may think that snow would be rather a cold sort of blanket? But in fact it is such a poor conductor of heat that the plants under it manage to survive in quite comfortable conditions. But on the British uplands things can be very different. Only on the highest Scottish mountains is there any reliable snow-lie. Farther south the snow usually comes and goes all through winter and seldom lies long. For this reason life can be more difficult for plants of southern mountains than it is further north. Fortunately mountain plants have other answers to bad weather besides relying on protection by snow.

For one thing they never grow tall, because snow would soon break them down if they did. They also have to keep their heads low to escape the worst of the winds that tear over the summits on many days throughout the year. So they grow as many mosses grow, in the shape of cushions formed of short stems crowding together to shelter each other. Moss campion and trailing azalea are examples. Others, such as lichens, liverworts, dwarf willow and mountain avens, also crouch low, spreading out as mats. One group, some of the saxifrages for instance, grow with their leaves flat on the ground in rosette shapes. Some are perennials which die down in autumn, leaving only their roots alive: in this group are alpine meadow-rue, alpine saw-wort, mountain sorrel, northern bedstraw (*Galium boreale*), parsley fern and many others.

Now let us look at another problem, one which plants face in summer—the problem of breeding or reproduction. On mountains summer is a short season and sometimes a poor one as well, with little sunshine and prolonged coolness and rain. In that sort of weather probably all plants find it harder to produce a new generation. But those in greatest difficulty are the annuals. They live for one summer only, shed their seed, then die. To keep their place as members of the mountain community these annuals need to produce at least a little good seed every year without fail. Inevitably very few annuals have succeeded in establishing themselves at high levels on our mountains. Alpine gentian (*Gentiana nivalis*), a beautiful but rare plant of Scottish mountains, is one of the few examples of summit annuals.

Some perennial mountain plants seem to have quite given up trying to produce seed and have gone in for other methods of reproduction. For instance, the very rare drooping saxifrage (*Saxifraga cernua*) is usually reluctant to flower: instead it forms little bulbs (called bulbils) in the angles where its uppermost leaves join the stem. When ripe these bulbils fall to the ground to become next year's plants if they survive. A very common species, the fir clubmoss (*Lycopodium selago*), also reproduces itself this way instead of by spores. High on mountains you may come upon grasses and certain other plants that look very odd: where you would expect to find their flowers or their seed heads you see what look like seedlings growing. Eventually these infant plants become detached from the parent and fall to the ground, where some of them take root. The grass called viviparous fescue (*Festuca vivipara*) is the commonest plant to reproduce itself in this way. 'Viviparous' means giving birth to living young as distinct from producing seeds or, in animals, laying eggs. The common lizard, which is found up to about 600 m (1970 ft) on British uplands, is viviparous: its young hatch from the egg just before they are born.

To see the greatest stretch of continuous arctic-alpine vegetation in

97

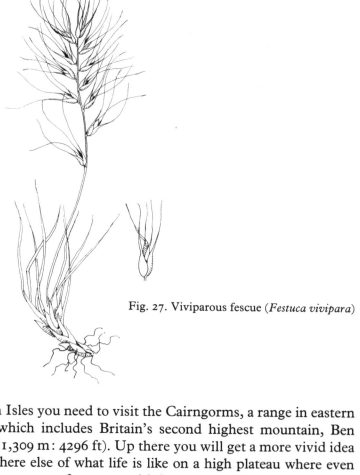

Fig. 27. Viviparous fescue (*Festuca vivipara*)

the British Isles you need to visit the Cairngorms, a range in eastern Scotland which includes Britain's second highest mountain, Ben Macdhui (1,309 m: 4296 ft). Up there you will get a more vivid idea than anywhere else of what life is like on a high plateau where even in summer you can often meet with low temperatures, tempests and heavy rain. In winter it can be truly severe. You will see how few are the species which can survive in those high bleak places on soil that is thin, acid, raw, infertile and insecure. Often there is no plant life at all—just bare, stony ground so disturbed by the action of frost that no roots can take hold in it. Where there is vegetation it is all very lowly—grey, shaggy spreads of woolly hair-moss (*Rhacomitrium lanuginosum*), mini-shrubs such as dwarf cornel (*Chamaepericly-menum suecicum*) and bog bilberry, the lichen mis-named reindeer moss (*Cladonia rangiferina*), and flowering plants called stiff sedge

98

(*Carex bigelowii*), three-leaved rush (*Juncus trifidus*), alpine lady's mantle (*Alchemilla alpina*) and Highland cudweed (*Gnaphalium norvegicum*). On the Cairngorms you will best see the effects of slowly melting snow, which for many weeks in summer is a source of water not only to mosses and liverworts but also to flowering plants such as alpine speedwell (*Veronica alpina*), arctic mouse-ear (*Cerastium arcticum*), Highland saxifrage (*Saxifraga rivularis*), starry saxifrage (*Saxifraga stellaris*), alpine willowherb (*Epilobium anagallidifolium*) and others which reappear as the snow cover shrinks.

But the Cairngorms are largely of granite and only here and there are its crags lime-rich and a haven for much variety in the flora. Other Scottish mountains, though not forming such a vast spread of high ground, are far wealthier in plants and none more so than the celebrated heights of Breadalbane near Perth, notably Ben Lawers, a National Nature Reserve where base-rich rocks are widespread and where arctic-alpines are in greater profusion than anywhere in the British Isles.

Just as the receding Ice Age left communities of arctic-alpine plants isolated on our mountains so it also stranded relict populations of insects and other small creatures. For an example we might take the mountain ringlet butterfly (*Erebia epiphron*), a very hardy species which presumably entered south Britain with the spread of the arctic-alpine vegetation and advanced north as the ice retreated. Then as the climate continued to get less cold this butterfly's range steadily narrowed until today it is found only very locally on some northern mountains. The same explanation probably goes also for the netted mountain moth (*Epelis carbonaria*), the black mountain moth (*Psodos coracina*), the northern dart (*Amathes alpicola*), the broad-bordered white underwing (*Anarta melanopa*), the mountain burnet (*Zygaena exulans*) and others which live high on mountains. So it is with almost any group of insects you choose to study: whether it is sawflies, craneflies, midges, stoneflies, beetles or other groups, you will find certain species that are found only on mountains. The same with spiders (*Araneae*) and other small fauna. But when you are searching for these high-level species you should bear in mind that animals are more mobile than plants and that most of those which live on mountains are to be found in the lowlands as well.

When we look at the mammals and birds of mountains we have to distinguish those which are true mountain species from those which have taken to the upland life because of human interference. The red deer, for instance, is so typical of mountains and moorlands it is easy to assume that the uplands were its orginal habitat. Yet this deer is more truly a woodland species (on the Continent it still is) and has taken to the open hills because man has so destroyed the once widespread hillside forests.

Fortunately red deer have been able to adapt to a variety of habitats, eating different plants according to the season and moving up and down the mountains with the weather. But it is the open grasslands that are now most important to them. There they eat not only fescues, bents and sweet vernal-grass as sheep do, but also coarser kinds like mat-grass and purple moor-grass. They also eat more sedges and rushes than sheep do and even clubmosses and lichens. Many of Scotland's high heather moors and grasslands, especially those amid wild and rocky country north-west of the Great Glen, have long been reserved as deer forests. 'Forest' in this sense has nothing to do with trees but simply means a hunting ground where deer are stalked by people with rifles. How much land should be occupied by deer and how much by sheep has caused many a bitter argument between deer-forest owners and sheep farmers.

The raven, a typical mountain-crag bird, is, like the red deer, a refugee. Because you see ravens quite commonly on high ground you should not think of them as especially adapted to arctic-alpine conditions. They are a relict population of a bird which was a widespread nester in woodlands all over the British lowlands until man succeeded in wiping them out in many districts. At first sight the golden eagle too, because almost restricted to the Scottish uplands and islands, may seem to be rather an alpine species. But there is little doubt that, like the raven and several carnivorous mammals such as wild cat and pine marten, the golden eagle would be more widespread in Britain, even in the lowlands, if man's hand were not so keenly against it.

Some of the small mammals of the lowlands are abundant also on mountains, notably wood mouse, field vole, common shrew and pygmy shrew. In Chapter 5 I mentioned field vole plagues in grassland newly enclosed for conifer plantations. Such plantations are not at great heights but on the Cairngorms at over 900 m (2950 ft) the grass has been reported to be severely attacked by voles. These small mammals survive the cold at high altitudes by burrowing under snow. Not that this saves them all: some are no doubt dug out by foxes for they too live on the high ground all through winter.

Three birds, all in Scotland, can be classed as truly alpine: ptarmigan, dotterel (*Eudromias morinellus*) and snow bunting. Of these only the ptarmigan is numerous, widespread and an all-year-round resident. It feeds mainly on shoots of heather, bilberry and other shrubs as well as on seeds, fruits and insects. For winter shelter ptarmigan dig holes in the snow as rodents, hares and foxes do. Only in very severe weather do they come down off the high ground altogether until the worst is over. The dotterel, a species of plover, also inhabits (but in spring and summer only) the summit zone of dwarf shrubs, short grasslands and stony ground with mosses and lichens, nesting in June on bare patches sometimes amid unmelted snowfields. Its food is largely craneflies, beetles, flies, insect larvae and spiders. The dotterel (less than a hundred pairs breed) is one of Britain's rare birds; it is also unusual in that the males do most of the incubating and rearing of the young. Dotterels have been found breeding at over 1,200 m (3940 ft). So too have snow buntings; for their breeding places they choose the very bleakest places of the mountains where the ground may be quite barren. But then the snow bunting is one of the hardiest birds in the world: in the Arctic it nests nearer the North Pole than any other species. No doubt snow buntings were widespread in Britain in colder ages. Now, as a breeding species, they are extremely rare. As migrants from the Continent in autumn and winter they become widespread in the British Isles, on uplands and coasts alike.

Ptarmigan, dotterel and snow bunting are not quite the highest birds of mountains if we include those which habitually fly over the summits. Swifts (*Apus apus*), for instance. Any fine day in summer before mid-August you may see swifts arrowing over the tops, far

Fig. 28. Ptarmigan (*Lagopus mutus*)

from their lowland breeding places. More than any other birds they make use of the great weather systems which bring massive air movements sweeping up over the mountains carrying multitudes of flying insects with them. The swifts ascend with these upward currents, feeding on flies all the way. And they travel at such headlong speeds they can be back with food at their nests down in the valleys in a very short time.

A real mountain bird, though we must call its habitats sub-alpine rather than alpine, is the ring ouzel, for it breeds almost throughout highland Britain, mainly between about 300 m (985 ft) and 600 m (1970 ft). It belongs most typically to heathery crags and so is very much a bird of the corries. And as you scramble about corries looking for ring ouzels you are pretty sure to find wrens as well and hear their loud song among the rocks. Wrens breed commonly up to about 600 m (1970 ft) and escape the worst of the mountain weather by retiring into crevices, caves and screes till it blows over.

Perhaps in thinking about our arctic-alpine plants and animals we might ask this question about them: what is likely to be their future?

As the Ice Age recedes further into the past are they going to find life getting ever more difficult until they vanish entirely from the British scene? Or will another Ice Age arrive in time to save them? To these questions we have no answer. Some weather experts tell us the climate is slowly getting colder. Others say there is insufficient evidence for this claim. The difficulty in all these predictions is that climate does not change steadily but by a series of fluctuations and it is impossible for us to be sure whether our climate is fluctuating towards colder or warmer conditions.

A far more immediate problem facing the mountain world is a conservation one. In these days of swift travel and much leisure more and more people are visiting the uplands and so pressure on high-level habitats is increasing rapidly. Under 'pressure' we can include everything from disturbance to actual damage to ground and vegetation by thousands of boots. Hill walkers inevitably converge towards the peaks and it is on and around the popular summits that overcrowding is greatest, especially where trains (as on Snowdon) or lifts (as on Cairngorm) carry people up in crowds.

The threats to the environment caused by these concentrations of people on mountain tops look like keeping conservationists busy for many years to come. So when you next go to the mountains think hard about these problems and try to work out possible solutions.

10. Studying a Mountain

There is no end to the interesting projects you can carry out on mountains. But whatever you choose to do you must plan it carefully so that you have a simple clear aim and a well thought out method of approach. And make sure you are properly equipped for the weather. Treat every mountain with respect and never go mountaineering either alone or in a party that has no experienced leader. You must have a detailed map with you and know how to read it. Also a compass and a whistle (six loud blasts repeated at one-minute intervals will probably bring help if you need it).

Remember that mountain weather can change very quickly. You may set off in a heat-wave in the valley yet feel nearly frozen on the summit because mist has come down or the wind has risen. So always carry spare clothing and wear proper mountain footwear. As well as your day's food have some emergency rations with you in case you are out longer than you intended. If the forecast is for bad weather then postpone your trip until it improves.

Before you set out it is very important to tell someone reliable what your route is going to be and where you intend to spend the night. Then keep to your plan. It is just as easy to have an accident on a British mountain as it would be on Everest. So don't take unnecessary risks and never try to move about on a mountain after dark. If possible get some initial training in mountain craft at a mountaineering centre. (See p. 115.)

Every district has its Naturalists' Trust or natural history societies. Perhaps you could join one as an individual member or as one of a group and go out on field excursions—an excellent way of learning about a region. (For addresses see pp. 114–15.)

Here are a few suggestions for projects:

Land use study
Choose a particular mountain to study, preferably one you can visit several times. Draw a map of it, marking the chief heights and contours and also the lakes, rivers, villages, hamlets, farms, roads and paths. Indicate the main features of the vegetation such as woodland, heather moor, peat bog and so on. Find out all you can about the land use (e.g. type of farming, forestry, quarrying or other industries) and mark these by symbols. Make your map as large as practicable so that you can go on adding all sorts of interesting details. Based on your own careful observations and also on what you've been able to find out by intelligent questions, a map of this sort can be a unique storehouse of knowledge.

Ice Age project
This is an exercise for detectives. What you're going out to find is as much evidence as possible that your mountain was once covered by great sheets of moving ice. Look for perched boulders, ice-smoothed rocks, glacial scratches, boulder clay, moraines, corries, glacier-formed lakes, U-shaped valleys with their tributary hanging valleys and all other signs of the Ice Age. Make drawings or take photographs of these features and mark them on a map.

Plant studies
Choose a square metre of vegetation such as grassland, peat bog, lakeside or scree and find out what you can about the numbers and distribution of its plants. Decide which are dominant, which are fairly common and which are uncommon. Then compare this area with other square metres nearby and record how the plants vary from one to another and try to decide why.

The height to which plants range is also worth looking at. As you climb your mountain make about half a dozen stops to compile a list of the plants near the track. Note how the species change as you go up and how few there are at the summit. If the mountain is a high one look out for alpine plants and the various ways in which they face up to the harsh conditions of life at the top.

Mammal studies
Equipped with a set of live traps you can sample the populations of voles and fieldmice in various habitats. There is scope for original research here because little is known about populations at high levels. One small mammal whose distribution is easily investigated is the mole: plot mole hills on a map and see how their distribution varies with different types, heights and aspects of grassland. Keep an eye open for signs of fox, badger, stoat, weasel and other predators; and for the tracks of deer, distinguishing these carefully from those of sheep. Whenever possible make plaster casts of any tracks you're not sure of: you may be able to identify them later.

Bird studies
Choose two or three common upland species such as skylark, meadow pipit, wheatear or whinchat and, taking care not to disturb either birds or nests, find out all you can about their habitat preferences, food, size of territories, population density, movements and other habits. Birds suitable for study in upland broad-leaved woods might be carrion crow, buzzard, redstart, wood warbler, tree pipit or pied flycatcher (*Ficedula hypoleuca*). If you have access to private woodland you might get permission to put nest boxes on the trees to find out how many are occupied by the different species and with what success. (Nest boxes should never be placed where the public can get at them: they are too liable to be vandalised).

If you can visit your study area in all seasons then bird counts can be of interest, showing the population changes that go on round the year. Another useful type of survey is to census the birds of different habitats so that you can make a comparison between the numbers living on heather moor, for instance, with those on, say, a newly planted conifer plantation.

Insect study
Make a note of all insects seen and record carefully which habitat they

25. An abandoned upland lead mine. Some old mines have unusual plants growing on the mineral-rich spoil heaps. Mines can also be a source of water pollution.

were in, date and time, weather conditions, numbers and any special observations about what they were doing. Then at the end of the day make a complete list divided into habitats so that you can see how these compare as living quarters for insects. Include spiders, woodlice (*Isopoda*), centipedes (*Chilopoda*), millepedes (*Diplopoda*), slugs and snails (*Mollusca*), etc., because, though not insects, they all add to the picture of small invertebrate life on the mountains.

Streams and lakes

Examine the water in different habitats. Does the temperature change much during the day? Does it seem to have plenty of oxygen in it or is it stagnant and lifeless? Is the bed stony, muddy, peaty or what? Are there any possible sources of pollution such as old lead or copper mines? Use indicator papers to test whether the water is acid, neutral or alkaline. When you have found out what you can about the water you can then make various studies of the animals and plants living in it. What species are there? How common or rare are they? What sort of habitat are they found in? Which habitats have most species? Can you say why? Usually the higher you climb the fewer plants and animals you will find in the water. But even tiny pools on mountain tops may be worth looking at: they sometimes have water beetles, caddis larvae or other insects in them.

Forestry plantations

The best type to study is a spruce plantation in its earliest years, when the trees may be a home for certain birds, mammals and insects which will abandon the plantation when the spruces bush out into the impenetrable thicket stage. Birds are the easiest to study and the best time for this is the breeding season. Census the birds of two or three hectares of young spruces and then compare this figure with a census of the same area of nearby heather moor, grassland or mature spruces. Insects and small mammal populations can be studied on similar lines.

An interesting project can be made about the creation of an upland forest: how the ground is prepared, where its trees come from, how they are planted and cared for, what the problems are, how the roads are made for extracting the timber, what uses are made of the forest products and what sort of life it is to be a forester. Remember that the Forestry Commission has visitor centres where information can be obtained on all aspects of forestry. (For addresses see p. 114.)

Sheep farming

Sheep are so important in the world of a mountain that they would make a very interesting project. Shepherds are usually willing to talk about their sheep and will give you lots of information. Find out how many sheep there are to the hectare, whether they spend the winter on the uplands or not, when the lambs are born and how many. When are the sheep washed, dipped, sheared? When are the lambs sent to market? How much are they worth? What are the problems of sheep farming? What diseases can sheep get and how are they dealt with? If a sheep dies on the mountain is it buried? If not what happens to it?

Or you could concentrate more on the natural history of sheep. Which species of grass do they prefer? Do they thrive better on modern improved grassland? What do they eat besides grass? How intelligent are they? How long do they live? Can they swim? How much do they eat and drink? Do they ever stop eating? Do they sleep at night? Are they quarrelsome? Does each sheep have its own patch of ground and keep to it? Or are they nomadic? You will think of many more questions of your own once you've got going.

A project on peat
Find out all you can about what peat is, how it originated and what plants are contained in it. If there is peat in your survey area try to discover when it was last used for fuel and who used it, how it was cut, stacked, dried and carried away. If you are in a district where peat is still used you could see these processes in action and could sketch or photograph them. If you visit a peat bog make lists of all the species of plants and animals you are able to record. Look out for tree remains in peat cuttings. Are they pine, birch or what? At what height are the highest tree remains that you can find? Find out all you can about ancient pollen preserved in peat and look out for illustrations of the different pollen grains.

Trackways
Every upland region has its disused trackways and these all have an interesting story to tell if you can discover it. Old maps are a great help in finding these roads, and so are aerial photographs if you can get hold of any from some library or museum. Trackways may be long-distance prehistoric ways or Roman roads. Or they may be medieval trade routes, links between monasteries or castles, military roads, cattle-droving roads, tracks to disused mines or quarries, former timber extraction roads, farm roads, peat roads and so on. Find out all you can from local people, parish histories and county archivists. You may well make some original discoveries because

many of these trackways are so ancient that no one is now sure of their purpose. They could lead you to the site of some long-lost upland settlement.

Final note
Even when you are mountaineering just for fun, always take a notebook with you, keep your eyes open and write down on-the-spot reports about anything you find interesting or puzzling about the rocks, the soils, the shape of the land, the weather, plants, insects, birds, mammals, anything at all. Get into the habit of thinking about mountains—what they are made of, how they got there, what makes one different from another. In this way you will find you have opened a door into a fascinating world.

Further Reading

Safety

The British Mountaineering Council. *Safety on Mountains.*
The Scout Association. *Safety on the Hills.*

Identification Books

Bang, P. and Dahlstrom, P. (1974) *Collins Guide to Animal Tracks and Signs.* Collins.

Brightman, F. H. and Nicholson, B. E. (1966) *The Oxford Book of Flowerless Plants.* O.U.P.

Brink, F. H. Van Den (1967) *A Field Guide to the Mammals of Britain and Europe.* Collins.

Burton, John (1968) *The Oxford Book of Insects.* O.U.P.

Campbell, Bruce (1972) *The Oxford Book of Birds.* O.U.P.

Chinery, M. (1973) *A Field Guide to the Insects of Britain and Northern Europe.* Collins.

Clegg, J. (1967) *The Observer's Book of Pond Life.* Warne.

Evans, I. O. (1971) *The Observer's Book of Geology.* Warne.

Fitter, R., Fitter, A. and Blamey, H. (1974) *The Wild Flowers of Britain and Northern Europe.* Collins.

Jewell, Arthur L. (1964) *The Observer's Book of Mosses and Liverworts.* Warne.

Kershaw, K. A. and Alvin, K. L. (1963) *The Observer's Book of Lichens.* Warne.

Lawrence, M. J. and Brown, R. (1967) *Mammals of Britain: their tracks, trails and signs.* Blandford.

Leutscher, Alfred (1960) *Tracks and Signs of British Animals.* Cleaver-Hume Press.

Mitchell, Alan (1974) *A Field Guide to the Trees of Britain and Northern Europe*. Collins.

Nichols, D. and Cooke, J. A. L. (1971) *The Oxford Book of Invertebrates*. O.U.P.

Peterson, R., Mountfort, G. and Hollom, P. A. D. (1974) *A Field Guide to the Birds of Britain and Europe*. Collins.

Southern, H. N. (1964) *The Handbook of British Mammals*. Blackwell.

Wells, A. L. (1941) *The Observer's Book of Freshwater Fishes*. Warne.

The 'Young Specialist' series (Burke) includes several very useful natural history guides.

Books about the Natural History of the Uplands

Bell, Mervyn (ed.) (1975) *Britain's National Parks*. David & Charles.

Condry, William (1966) *The Snowdonia National Park*. Collins.

Condry, William (1974) *Woodlands*. Collins.

Darling, F. Fraser and Boyd, J. Morton (1964) *The Highlands and Islands*. Collins.

Edlin, H. L. (1956) *Trees, Woods and Man*. Collins.

Edwards, K. C. (1962) *The Peak District*. Collins.

Harvey, L. A. and Leger-Gordon, D. St. (1962) *Dartmoor*. Collins.

Hervey, G. A. K. and Barnes, J. A. G. (1970) *Natural History of the Lake District*. Warne.

National Trust for Scotland (1964) *Ben Lawers and its alpine flowers*.

Nethersole-Thompson, D. (1951) *The Greenshank*. Collins.

—— (1966) *The Snow Bunting*. Oliver & Boyd.

—— (1973) *The Dotterel*. Collins.

—— (1975) *Pine Crossbills*. Poyser.

Nethersole-Thompson, D. and Watson, Adam (1974) *The Cairngorms*. Collins.

Pearsall, W. H. (1972) *Mountains and Moorlands*. Collins.

Pearsall, W. H. and Pennington, W. (1973) *The Lake District*. Collins.

Raistrick, A. (1965) *The Face of North-West Yorkshire*. Dalesman.

Raven, John and Walters, Max (1956) *Mountain Flowers*. Collins.

Schofield, Peter (1975) *Exploring Woods*. Independent Television

Books Ltd.

Stamp, L. Dudley (1970) *Britain's Structure and Scenery.* Collins.

Steele, R. C. (1972) *Wildlife Conservation in Woodlands.* Forestry Commission Booklet 29.

Stephen, David (1963) *Watching Wild Life.* Collins.

Tansley, A. G. (1968) *Britain's Green Mantle* (Revised by M. C. F. Proctor). Allen & Unwin.

Trueman, A. E. (1972) *Geology and Scenery in England and Wales.* Penguin.

Other Sources of Information

There is an ever increasing number of centres in or near highland Britain which provide information and exhibits on many aspects of the countryside including natural history. For further details apply to the following organisations:

The British Tourist Authority, 64 St. James's Street, London SW1A 1NF
(Nature trails, etc.)

The Council for Nature, Zoological Gardens, Regent's Park, London, NW1 4RY
(General information about the conservation of nature in Britain.)

The Countryside Commission, John Dower House, Crescent Place, Cheltenham, Glos. GL50 3RA
(National Parks, visitor centres, long-distance footpaths, etc.)

The Forestry Commission, 25 Savile Row, London W1X 2AY
(Nature trails, visitor centres, literature and teachers' packs.)

The National Trust, 42 Queen Anne's Gate, London SW1, and the National Trust for Scotland, 5 Charlotte Square, Edinburgh EH2 4DU
(These Trusts own much land open to the public in highland Britain.)

The Nature Conservancy Council, 19 Belgrave Square, London SW1X 8PY
(Information centres, literature, nature trails, National Nature Reserves.)

The Royal Society for the Protection of Birds, The Lodge, Sandy, Bedfordshire SG19 2DL
(RSPB Reserves, The Young Ornithologists' Club, outdoor courses, literature.)

The Society for the Promotion of Nature Reserves, The Green, Nettleham, Lincoln
(Information about the Naturalists' Trusts and their reserves.)

The Youth Hostels Association, Trevelyan House, St. Albans, Herts. AL1 2DY
(Some hostels specialise in natural history courses.)

Natural history courses are available at the various field study centres of the Field Studies Council, Preston Montford, Montford Bridge, Shrewsbury SY4 1HW, and of the Scottish Field Studies Association, Forelands, 18 Marketgate, Crail, Fife, KT10 3TL.

There are also many other centres where you can receive instruction in natural history. Details of these can be found in:

The Directory of Centres for Outdoor Studies in England and Wales published by the Council for Environmental Education, School of Education, 24 London Road, Reading RG1 5HE

For information about centres in Scotland apply to:
The Secretary, The Scottish Committee on Education and the Countryside, 46 Munro Road, Jordanhill, Glasgow

Mountaineering courses are available at centres run by The Sports Council, 70 Brompton Road, London SW3 1EX

Many Museums have displays, collections and information about the geology and natural history of upland regions. Some also organise field excursions and lectures.

Index

INDEX

Aviemore, 42
Awl-wort, 86
Azalea, trailing, 94, 96

Bala Lake, 87
Badger, 53, 55
Base-rich (basic) soils, 91, 92, 95, 99
Bearberry, 42, 92, 94
   alpine, 92
Bedstraw, heath, 42, 58
   northern, 97
Beech, 36
Bees, honey, in heather, 73–4
Beetles, click, 61
   dor, 61
   heather, 74–5
   water, 81, 88
Beinn Eighe Reserve, 44
Ben Lawers, 99
Ben Macdhui, 98
Ben Nevis, 13, 62
Betula spp, (birch), 31, 33, 39, 40–1, 86
Bilberry, 33, 42, 72, 91, 92, 94
Bilberry, bog, 92, 98
Birchwoods, 31, 33, 39, 40–1, 86, Pl. 8
Bird study, 106
Blackbird, 37, 51
Blechnum spicant (hard fern), 38
Bluebell, 38, 39
Bogbean, 68, 85
Bogs *see* Peat bogs
Boulder clay, 29, Fig. 11
Bracken, 32–3, 39–40
Broom, 61
Bufo bufo (toad), 88
Bulbils, 97
Bullfinch, 51
Bullhead, 81
Bunting, snow, 64, 101
Burns, 80–81
Bur-reed, branched, 85
Buteo buteo (buzzard), 37, 49, 52, 62, 63
Butterflies:
   gatekeeper, 31
   green hairstreak, 61, Pl. 13
   large heath, 73
   large white, 73
   meadow brown, 31
   mountain ringlet, 99
   peacock, 31
   red admiral, 73
   Scotch argus, 61
   small heath, 61, 73
   small tortoiseshell, 31, 73
   speckled wood, 31
   wall, 31
Butterwort, Pl. 17
Buzzard, 37, 49, 52, 62, 63

Caddis flies, 81
Cairngorms, 62, 72, 76, 98, 99, 101, 103
Calcareous rocks, 91
Calcicoles, 91
Calcifuges, 91
Calcium, 89, 91
Calidris alpina (dunlin), 76
Callophrys rubi (green hairstreak), 61, Pl. 13
Calluna vulgaris (heather), 33, 65, 69, 71–7, 91, 92, 94
Campion, moss, 92, 95, 96
   red, 95
Capercaillie, 44, 46
Capreolus capreolus (roe deer), 44, 56, Fig. 14
Carduelis spinus (siskin), 41, 44, 52
Carex bigelowii (stiff sedge), 98
   C. rostrata (bottle sedge), 85
Carrion, 64
Cat, wild, 38, 55, 100
Cattle, 32, 33, 39
Centipedes, 107
Ceramica pisi (broom moth), 39, Pl. 7
Cerapteryx graminis (antler moth), 61
Cerastium arcticum (arctic mouse-ear), 99
Ceratopogonidae (midges), 74, 88
Certhia familiaris (tree creeper), 37
Cervus elaphus (red deer), 44, 76, 100, Fig. 14
Chaffinch, 37, 41, 51
Chamaepericlymenum suecicum (dwarf cornel), 98

118

INDEX

INDEX

INDEX